the **NO-NONSENSE** guide to

WORLD HISTORY

Chris Brazier

KU-749-998

The No-Nonsense Guide to World History
First published in the UK by
New Internationalist™ Publications Ltd
Oxford OX4 1BW, UK
www.newint.org
New Internationalist is a registered trade mark.

in association with
Verso
6 Meard Street
London
W1F 0EG
www.versobooks.com

Cover photo: Petroglyphs (Corbis/Stock Market)

Second edition printed 2002, reprinted 2003, 2004.

Design by Alan Hughes, New Internationalist Publications Ltd.
Series editor: Troth Wells

Printed by TJ International Ltd, Padstow, Cornwall, UK.

British Library Cataloguing in Publication Data.
A catalogue record for this book is available from the British Library.

Library of Congress Cataloguing-in-Publication Data.
A catalogue record for this book is available from the Library of Congress.

ISBN - 1 85984 355 7

the **NO-NONSENSE** guide to
WORLD HISTORY
Chris Brazier

About the author

Chris Brazier has been a co-editor of **New Internationalist** magazine since 1984. His previous publications include *Vietnam: The Price of Peace*. He is currently working on contract for the UN Children's Fund, *UNICEF*.

Other titles in the series

The No-Nonsense Guide to Globalization
The No-Nonsense Guide to Fair Trade
The No-Nonsense Guide to Climate Change
The No-Nonsense Guide to International Migration
The No-Nonsense Guide to Sexual Diversity
The No-Nonsense Guide to Democracy
The No-Nonsense Guide to Class, Caste & Hierarchies
The No-Nonsense Guide to The Arms Trade
The No-Nonsense Guide to International Development
The No-Nonsense Guide to Indigenous Peoples
The No-Nonsense Guide to Terrorism
The No-Nonsense Guide to World Poverty
The No-Nonsense Guide to HIV/AIDS
The No-Nonsense Guide to Global Media
The No-Nonsense Guide to Islam
The No-Nonsense Guide to Women's Rights
The No-Nonsense Guide to Water

Foreword

CHRIS BRAZIER is right; a historian confronting the task of a history of the world in forty thousand words would gasp. No professional is presented with this challenge, even in the most general first year outline course. Chris moves easily from the slimy origins of organisms to asymmetrical power relations in the twentieth century. His history is a **New Internationalist** history, linked with other themes being pursued in the *No-Nonsense Guide* series. He insists, as do many contemporary historians, that we should break away from Euro-centric interpretations and narratives. He demands that women's history be placed center stage. He reminds us constantly that in most epochs, and most cultures, there have been sharp inequalities: humankind faces this dilemma as starkly, perhaps more so, at the beginning of the 21st century. His history includes a record of extraordinary human movement and migration, a phenomenon with a long pedigree that remains central to contemporary concerns in a world with bounded nation states. Although he does not offer an environmental interpretation of history, he ends with a plea for environmental consciousness in facing core issues of humankind's reciprocal relationship with nature. We remain, after all, and before anything else – before our color or culture or religion – a mammal species dependent upon the natural world.

The human species is, however, unique, not least in its self-criticism. Chris Brazier's history is critical of many aspects of the past, and also of its interpretation by previous generations of Europeans. Here I agree with him, and this capacity to change and reassess must remain one of our culture's great strengths. There are also points where I may disagree with Chris. Everywhere he wishes to look behind the relics of pyramids, monuments and palaces and to investigate the human cost and the work involved. Yet his treatment of pre-colonial African empires is perhaps too celebratory, somewhat in contrast to his emphasis on hierarchy and exploitation in the pre-Columbian Latin America. Sometimes he does not correct enough for me. I can see why he has to focus on empires and politics in this history, in order to provide some chronological framework across vast swathes of time, but I would like to hear more loudly the voices of plain people. And perhaps I am less troubled by the future, the opportunities offered by the modern world and technology, and more convinced of the benefits of uneven, sometimes faltering, global democratisation.

Historians are a querulous bunch and are taught to be so. On no account should we be protected from brave generalisers who seek to make sense of the whole, when so many professionals cultivate close vision. History must inevitably be a subject for contestation, because it is always to some degree ideological in nature, and because it is so important for understanding, justifying or changing the present. This book is a challenge. It is vivid, informal and informative. Let us give it to schoolkids and students to read; let's listen to their comments. They will have their own interests which they would wish to find mirrored in the past. We must find ways to cater for them and this kind of text is a good place to start. Perhaps every professional historian should be required to write a history of the world in forty thousands words – nothing would be more conducive to humility.

Professor William Beinart
St Antony's College
University of Oxford

the **NO-NONSENSE** guide to
WORLD HISTORY

CONTENTS

Foreword by William Beinart 5

Introduction 8

1 In the beginning 10

2 Pharaohs and priestesses 17

3 Superpowers and barbarians 22

4 God and the spirit 27

5 Greek and Latin 32

6 The rise and rise of religion 39

7 Light in the East 46

8 Wars of the cross 52

9 Glory and murder in the New World 60

10 The hidden continent 68

11 Shadow of the Sun King 76

12 The American way 81

13 The power and plenty of Asia 88

14 Liberté, Egalité, Fraternité 92

15 Revolution 97

16 Carving up the world 102

17 Total war 111

18 The power of the workers 114

19 Capitalism and Fascism 117

20 The radical 20th century 124

Marking time: chronology 137

Index 144

the **NO-NONSENSE** guide to

WORLD HISTORY

THE BRIEFER a history of the world sets out to be, the more ambitious it inevitably is. Some people write entire learned tomes about postage stamp design between 1864 and 1902. So how can I possibly condense the whole history of the world into such a limited space? Only by being very selective and sweeping. But I think there is a real value to this. Many historians have an intimate knowledge of their particular nook or cranny but may not always stand back to try and see the great building in its entirety.

Indeed most of us know bits and pieces of history without ever knowing how they fit together. This came home to me when I was in the attic sorting through boxes of papers from my own ancient past. I came across the history projects I did at school. And almost all were about wars – pages and pages on the disposition of the Duke of Marlborough's troops at the Battle of Blenheim, whole chapters on the different phases of the Napoleonic Wars.

The energy I put into all this came from a certain fascination with the past – I wanted to be transported back into a bygone age to see how its people really lived. But what a waste of that enthusiasm to have it expended on military campaigns in a tiny corner of Europe when all the world and time was there for the tasting... School taught me next to nothing about the histories of Asia, Africa and Latin America. The odd queen aside, I learned nothing at all about women's history, which has been submerged for thousands of years beneath the endless flow of wars and politics and is only now beginning to surface. And I was taught very little about the everyday experience of ordinary people throughout the ages, the ones who actually died building the Pyramids or plowed the fields beneath the castle.

So researching this history, originally for an issue of the **New Internationalist** magazine, was a real adventure – as I delved into the continents and communities that were left out of all the old text books. But I have also tried to integrate these hidden histories with the more conventional narrative of imperial dynasties and superpower battles.

The contribution of ordinary women and men should never be overlooked, but history would be unintelligible if it did not include the politics and the conquering empires that have helped shape their world. History teachers may now try to give children a picture of the great world beyond their own shores. But this book is for all those of us who have only a few fragments of the tapestry.

Chris Brazier
Oxford

1 In the beginning

Humble beginnings. Life stirs in the mud pools and blossoms into fish, reptiles and finally mammals. Then humans take the stage and start to colonize the planet.

IN THE BEGINNING there was slime. Darwin's idea that humans might be descended from the apes outraged 19th-century Christians. But they hadn't grasped the half of it. Our original ancestors were actually a few slimy micro-organisms. And even they were latecomers on the scene. The earth had already existed in a lifeless state for at least five billion years after its first independent existence from the sun.

Millions of years passed and slime turned to jelly; then jelly to shellfish. Great sea scorpions were followed by backboned fish. This astonishing development of life, from the first stirrings in the mud to the vertebrate fish and beyond to reptiles and animals, was all governed by the process of natural selection. The creatures which survived best had a certain advantage: a sensitivity to light, perhaps, or a slightly more resilient outer shell. These reproduced more prolifically and ensured that life evolved in different directions – but always towards forms better adapted for survival.

Some creatures moved to the land, modifying their gills into lungs in order to breathe the oxygen in air instead of in water – and even now human babies in the womb have gills before they have lungs, in honor of that ancient evolutionary adaptation.

These were the reptiles, and the largest of them, the dinosaurs, were the dominant form of life on earth for 200 million years before dying out, possibly because the climate became much colder, from around 60 million years ago. Smaller creatures, which had adapted better to lower temperatures, then inherited the earth. These were birds who had grown feathers and warmed the eggs of their young; and primitive mammals who had fur and retained their babies inside the female body until they had matured.

There was social as well as physical evolution. Reptiles, lower down the evolutionary scale, simply abandoned their eggs – their offspring had to fend for themselves. But mammals nourished their young and so had a social and educational relationship with them. Useful information could be passed on and developed instead of every individual starting from instinctual scratch. Animals became interested in the company of other animals and formed herds or societies.

Five million years BC – Ancestral apes

The first mammals to approximate to the human form emerged out of the ape family in Central Africa about five million years ago. These *Australopithecines*, 'Southern apes', walked on two legs (and thus, vitally, gained the use of their hands). They became the first animals ever to make rudimentary tools by chipping stones to create a sharp edge, but the last of them died out a million years ago. They were superseded by other, even more human-like creatures with a more erect stature and a larger brain size, known by the Latin term *homo erectus*, which developed around one-and-a-half million years ago. Between 800,000 and 500,000 years ago *homo erectus* and *femina erecta* spread not only all over Africa but also into Europe and Asia, reaching as far afield as Java and Northern China. Their discovery of how to manage (though probably not create) fire made it possible for them to inhabit colder climates; and contrary to popular myth even these pre-humans constructed shelters from branches and stones more often than they lived in caves.

300,000 BC – Our mother Eve

These beings may seem primitive and remote. But all our family trees have their roots in these *erectus* pre-humans or hominids. An element of DNA – the genetic coding we all carry in our cells – has been traced back to a common ancestor, an African woman who lived about 300,000 years ago. Imagine her straining to give birth under a fierce sun on the savanna, little knowing that she was gifting her baby with a genetic blueprint that was to be carried by conquerors and concubines, atomic physicists and peace campaigners, through hundreds of thousands of years – to wind up being thought of here and now

The myth of Man the Hunter

The most popular image of the first humans is of the cave man, rough, tough and brutal, who channels his 'natural' aggression into killing animals for food and drags along (by her hair) the woman who cooks his food, gratifies his sexual urges and carries his children.

This has more to do with the fevered imaginations and wishful thinking of male experts than it does with the reality – an object lesson in the distortion of history by personal perspective. Ever since the first serious study of fossils and skeletons in the wake of Darwin, people have asked why human beings put all their evolutionary energy into the development of their brains rather than their bodies. And these experts have come back time and time again to hunting as the key to all human development, with evolution reduced to a physical battle between violent men.

According to popular zoologist, Desmond Morris, even the current arrangement of the female body is down to Man the Hunter. He believes that when the first hominids started to walk on two legs, men wanted frontal sex and women responded by growing breasts to arouse them, realizing that their buttocks were no longer enough. Breastfeeding is a much more plausible explanation.

Similarly US writer Robert Ardrey believes that the female orgasm was evolved as a reward for the tired hunter at the end of the day: women's own pleasure and thus incentive to propagate the species apparently had nothing to do with it. In scientific circles these ideas have now been discredited, though it will take a while for popular thinking to catch up.

The hunting and gathering peoples who have survived into our own time provide a more likely insight into the life of early humans. Hunting in these groups is conducted in 95 per cent of cases by men. But hunting itself cannot provide enough food, not least because dead flesh will not keep in the African climate – the !Kung San Bushmen of Botswana, for instance, hunted for only one week per month.

The rest of the time the !Kung and all other Stone-Age men ate the nuts, berries, herbs and grasses that women gathered. This indicates by me and you. In so far as we'll ever be able to trace things back: Eve not Adam, came first.

If the earth's life were seen as a single day, human beings proper would only appear in the last second before midnight – and from 40,000 years ago the newest human model (*homo sapiens*) spread all over the world. These early people lived by gathering and hunting. The normal phrase is 'hunting and gathering' and the emphasis is usually placed on the

that women would never have been dependent on men to bring home the bacon.

Food gathering required skills of memory and careful selection – as well as tools for digging. But an even more important contribution to the evolution of the human brain came from childcare. Human young take much longer to become self-supporting than apes and not just in a physical sense: they need to be taught about a far more complex society. The stimulation of children through play and activity must have added enormously to the development of the brain, just as it stimulates intelligence in infants now.

Hunting has been claimed as the key activity in human development, the one that allowed humans to survive and thrive, to inherit the earth. But a much more significant development took place entirely inside women's bodies – the shift from primate oestrus (when the female periodically comes on heat) to menstruation. The great female primates – chimpanzees, gorillas and orang-utans – come on heat rarely and produce one baby every five or six years. This puts them at risk and means they can only survive in a favorable environment.

With 12 chances of conceiving every year the human female has a much greater reproductive capacity and this enabled the species to survive even in the most hostile habitats. Naturally men played a great part in human development – it is only necessary to stress women's contribution because they have until now been utterly forgotten. Stone-Age culture was emphatically not like its cartoon image. Men were not savage killers, slavering with aggression. Their hunting was not solo heroism but rather a collective activity which usually involved trapping so as to avoid a battle. Women and men generally worked as partners, relying on each others' skills.

In a peculiar way the most useful cartoon image of the Stone Age is the one which is intentionally inaccurate, *The Flintstones*, because it suggests these people were not so very different from us.

Beware of the man who argues that the differences between women and men are inevitable, given the 'natural aggression' that made Stone Age Man a hunter. He is getting carried away by his own fantasies. ∎

hunting aspect, with the men going out to bring back slain animal carcasses for women to cook on the fire. In fact these early people would have eaten much more vegetable than animal matter – it was women who gathered the fruits, nuts and berries that sustained people most of the time. And if hunting and gathering peoples that still exist are anything to go by, these early humans probably had a deep respect for women and their contribution. Women had freedom of movement and were not sexually attached to one man. They could be counselors, leaders, doctors and law givers – and had their own special status as holders of the most sacred mystery of all, that of birth.

40,000-10,000 BC –
The first Australians and Americans

The hominids had only colonized Africa, Europe and Asia. But humans now reached out even farther and occupied the remaining continents of Australia and the Americas. They were helped by the climate. The world was still then in the grip of the last Ice Age with glaciers reaching as far south as what are now Berlin, London and Chicago. And this freezing reduced the sea level – just as global warming threatens to raise sea levels by melting polar ice now. As the sea receded, land bridges appeared.

So Australia, Papua New Guinea, Indonesia and the Philippines were all either joined or within a short boating distance of each other – and the first Australians set foot in the uninhabited continent some time during the last Ice Age. They were to spread throughout the land and establish their own independent cultural traditions, isolated from the rest of humanity for tens of thousands of years until European ships re-established contact.

At about the same time, groups of intrepid Asian nomads crossed another land bridge, that over the Bering Strait which now separates Siberia from Alaska. They spread through the wide open spaces of this rich new land and by the end of the Ice Age had established themselves in virtually every region of the Americas, from the frozen north through the deserts and tropical forests to the chilly tip of what is now Tierra del Fuego. Some time after this the sea rose again to cut off the two halves of the world and leave these early Americans to develop independently of their relations.

The world's population in this period was not more than ten million – the same as one of today's megacities. And by now the distribution of ethnic types by geographical region was probably quite close to the way modern people would think of them: black-skinned people in Africa, white- and brown-skinned people in Europe and India, and Mongoloid people in the Far East and the Americas. Natural selection was also responsible for this: Africans' dark skin, for instance, provides them with protection against the fierceness of tropical sunlight.

9,000 BC – Taming the earth
Most people continued to live by gathering and hunting – and some groups survive even now who have lived this way continuously since the Old Stone Age. Usually this was because their way of life was so integrated with their environment that they never needed to develop. The Amazonian indians that Westerners only recently encountered for the first time have been sustained by the jungle around them.

But populations in other parts of the world grew to the point where humans had to come up with a new way of getting food. One upshot was the taming of animals – sheep first, in northern Iraq around 9,000 BC, with goats, pigs and cattle following over the next couple of thousand years. But, even more significantly, people started to experiment with the crops they had hitherto gathered wild. The first cultivation of millet and rice probably took place in southeast Asia around 10,000 BC but more is known about the development of domesticated crops in the Near East: wheat and barley had spread throughout that region by 7,000 BC and to the Indus Valley (modern Pakistan) just after. Growing an agricultural surplus meant that the first towns could emerge. The earliest known was the Palestine settlement of Jericho, which was a small village in 9,000 BC but had by a thousand years later become a town of mud-bricked houses covering an area of at least seven acres (three hectares).

5,000 BC – Ancient inequality

All kinds of changes occurred when people gathered in towns. Diseases like measles and tuberculosis could now be spread more easily, and life expectancy at this point was probably as little as 30 years for women and 35 for men – though before we start feeling superior we should remember that this is little different from the 39 years people can expect to live in modern Malawi and Sierra Leone.

But urban life also created a new kind of society. Nomadic peoples had little use for possessions, since they would only have to carry them. Settled people, on the other hand, almost immediately began to fire pottery and work in copper and gold. These beautiful things soon became symbols of rank and status and a gap began to emerge between rich and poor, together with a separation between social classes based on different kinds of work. Inequality was one of the first results of living in towns – and we have still not outgrown it.

2 Pharaohs and priestesses

The first civilizations appear and begin to display an aspiring intelligence – and an appalling readiness to hold whole groups of people in permanent subjection.

CIVILIZATION. Literally it means people living together in towns and cities. But 'civilized' has come to connote much more: the highest human virtues. Like most words, it gains its meaning from what it opposes: barbarism. Human beings tend to dismiss other people's way of life as inferior or primitive. And people in the first towns and cities considered those still dependent on gathering food to be ignorant and aggressive. But 'civilization' had introduced its own barbarities: institutionalized warfare and slavery.

The first real civilization had appeared by 3,500 BC in Sumer, a land lying between the Tigris and Euphrates rivers in what is now Iraq. And a separate development followed little more than a hundred years later in Egypt. The Sumerians and Egyptians have traditionally been seen as the progenitors of civilization, locked together in a kind of Special Development Zone. It has suited traditional historians to think of the Mediterranean as the source of all major human developments, mainly because modern Western culture has its roots there.

But we have recently discovered that the first Egyptians were actually Africans from the middle of the Sahara. Many of these migrated to Egypt when their own fertile lands began to dry up after about 4,000 BC.

Others headed south to the forests of West Africa and this explains the many similar traditions between the two regions. The idea of kingship is traditionally attributed to Egypt but is in fact African – archaeologists have discovered that a succession of 12 kings ruled the state of Nubia in modern Sudan before there was ever a Pharaoh.

3,000 BC – Asian pioneers

History has concentrated on the Mediterranean and neglected the early civilizations of India and China. Yet the Indians were in many ways much more advanced than the Egyptians. They dominated, from their base in the Indus Valley, an empire of about 500,000 square miles (1.25 million square kilometers) – compared to Egypt's 15,500/40,000. And their cities like Harappa were laid out on a meticulous grid system with elaborate drainage.

The Great Goddess

In the beginning God was a woman. For at least 25,000 years people worshipped the Mother of All Things. The Father God of Judaism, Christianity and Islam has been revered for only a tenth of that time.

The worship of the Great Goddess emerged out of woman's clear link with nature: the way she produced blood in perfect rhythm with the cycles of the moon. Even more magical and vital was her production of children, since people did not understand men's part in this miraculous process – some Aboriginal peoples, for instance, believed that spirit children dwelt in pools and trees and entered women at random when they wished to be born. So it seemed natural to believe that one great mother had brought the world into being. Thus the Babylonian goddess Ishtar was herself the cosmic uterus, while in Roman mythology Gaia, the Mother Earth, emerged from a primal vagina, the abyss of all-feeling and all-knowing.

But this Great Goddess oversaw death as well as birth. And she could demand sacrifice in return for co-operation. Often this was a sexual sacrifice, since the Goddess had a voracious sexual appetite – the fruitfulness of crops and animals was only ever a by-product of the Goddess's own sexual activity and enjoyment. So in many cultures a beautiful young man was sacrificed to her each year – 'king' was originally an honorary title given to this man. The Assyrian goddess Anaitis was honored each year by the most beautiful boy, who would be painted and clothed in red and gold and spend a last day and night having sex with her priestesses in full public view. He would then be covered with a cloth of gold and set on fire.

This did not always mean that women held power on earth – there was no age of matriarchy as a mirror image of the later patriarchy – though examples of woman power abound. Queen Sammuramat of Assyria, for instance, ruled as regent from 810 to 805 BC and passed into myth as the Warrior Goddess Semiramis. In ancient Egypt dynastic power passed through the woman even when the pharoah was male.

But their greatest achievements were in shipbuilding. Their three or four-masted vessels could make the greatest possible use of the wind, 3,000 years before Europeans came up with such technology. They probably sailed in these right across the Pacific; woven cotton from the Peru of 2,500 BC has been traced back to cotton strains cultivated by the Harappans.

In China, meanwhile, the first city-based empire, that of the Shang dynasty from around 1,700 BC, extended over 250,000 square miles (647,500 square

Eventually, though, the Great Goddess was dethroned by male gods. This took place over hundreds, even thousands, of years at a different pace in each culture. The starting-point was usually men's discovery of their role in birth. But the change was also linked with social factors. For thousands of years women were responsible for growing food through horticulture.

But about 6,000 BC an upsurge in population caused a shift to more intensive agriculture, which saw Nature as having to be tamed. Men took on this role, plowing and sowing the passive fields in the same way as they saw themselves acting to women (hence the word 'husbandry'). And the more military became the organization of urban society, the more men with their greater physical strength gained the upper hand.

But whatever the reason, the phallus now became the focus of worship, the sacred source of all that lived. Phallic pillars proliferated in Greece, and in India Shiva achieved dominance over the other two main gods just by the size of his organ – for thousands of years the priest of Shiva came out naked ringing a bell to call women to kiss his holy genitals.

So the Goddess was deposed. This revolution is represented in most mythologies, which begin with a Great Mother Creator but then see her son or lover gaining more and more power until eventually he rules alone. In the simplest mythological version, that of the Semitic Babylonians, the god-king Marduk wages war on Ti'amat, Mother of all Things, and hacks her to pieces. He forms the world from the pieces of her body.

The Kikuyu of Kenya recall how their male ancestors overthrew women by raping them all on the same day and mastering them nine months later. In an Aztec ceremony every December a woman dressed up as Ilamtecuhtli, the old goddess of earth and corn, was decapitated and her head presented to a priest wearing her costume and mask.

But this was only the beginning: in the 1,200 years between 600 BC and 600 AD five major religions came into being, all based on the divine word of one man. From then on male power was more enshrined than ever and the age of patriarchy began. ■

kilometers). The Shang were probably the nomadic conquerors of people around the Yellow River who had already been growing rice for over 2,000 years, and millet for 3,000.

2,500 BC – Hard labor and megalomania
These earliest civilizations were spectacular developments. For ordinary people in all these

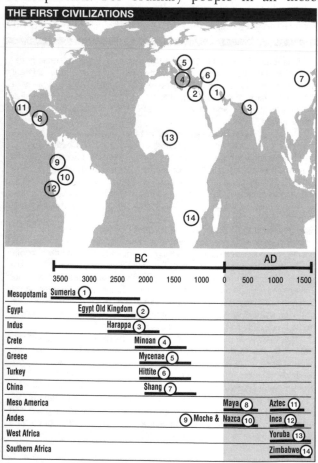

THE FIRST CIVILIZATIONS

	BC						AD		
	3500	3000	2500	2000	1500	1000	0	500	1000	1500
Mesopotamia	Sumeria ①								
Egypt			Egypt Old Kingdom ②						
Indus				Harappa ③					
Crete				Minoan ④					
Greece				Mycenae ⑤					
Turkey				Hittite ⑥					
China				Shang ⑦					
Meso America								Maya ⑧	Aztec ⑪
Andes						⑨ Moche & Nazca ⑩			Inca ⑫
West Africa									Yoruba ⑬
Southern Africa									Zimbabwe ⑭

Based on information in the *Third World Atlas*, Open University 1994 empires, though, life would have been pretty similar. The majority would have lived simply by cultivating the fields, trading only occasionally through barter. But sometimes they were required to risk their lives in war against another state or abandon their own cultivation to labor for the greater glory of their rulers: thousands of ordinary Egyptians died erecting the Great Pyramids of Gizeh, each for a different megalomaniac Pharaoh who wished to outdo his predecessor.

2,000 BC – Religion and writing

When farmers were able to produce more food than they themselves needed, others were able to specialize in different crafts and professions. One of the first to emerge was that of the priesthood. In the early civilizations priests were usually female. And so was God. From 25,000 BC the worship of the Great Goddess Mother was practised all over the world, from the steppes of southern Russia to Australia.

Women's status was thus much more equal than it is today: in Egypt a wife was so financially independent that if her husband borrowed money from her she could charge interest; in the marriage ceremony the husband pledged never to oppose his wife's wishes.

The first known writing in the world appeared on the Temple of the Goddess in the Sumerian city of Uruk (the Bible's Erech). Writing probably developed independently in each civilization, since the forms it took were distinct: both the Egyptians and the Chinese relied to some extent on pictorial representations while the Sumerians had something closer to the common modern conception of abstract symbols. And it is to these earliest civilizations that we owe our own measurement of time: the Sumerians divided the hour into 60 minutes and the minute into 60 seconds; while the Egyptians divided the year into 365 days. Little did they realize how dominated by those hours and minutes their descendants would prove to be.

3 Superpowers and barbarians

City states become empires and develop pointless warfare to a high art. They fear the nomadic peoples around them – often with good reason.

NOMADIC GROUPS STILL wandered the wide world beyond the first civilizations. In the Americas and Australia, and in Africa south of the Sahara, the nomads had no idea that any other lifestyle existed. Nomadic people in Europe and Asia had more contact with settled societies. They followed their herds from summer to winter pastures and constructed a social life around that seasonal movement. They lived in their own clan units but could be broadly split into three important groups. The Mongolian peoples roamed the grasslands of central Asia and were skilled with horses; the Semitic peoples used the deserts of Arabia to rear goats and sheep; and the Aryans occupied much of Europe.

2,400 BC – Nomadic conquerors

The Semitic peoples were the first to have an impact on the settled civilizations. They were great sailors. One group, the Phoenicians, set up trading cities such as Tyre, Sidon and Carthage all over the Mediterranean. But they were also warriors: Semitic people started raiding and then conquering Sumerian city states and by 2,400 BC their leader Sargon ruled the whole of Sumer. Later waves of Semitic invaders gradually established Babylon as their capital. Around 1,800 BC the Babylonian empire was consolidated by a king, Hammurabi, who codified the first set of laws we know about. Many seem very advanced today, not least because they treated women and men as equals: the law said that a woman's dowry should be given to her on marriage and that this, together with her own land and property, should remain hers until death; also women could divorce men on the grounds of cruelty, after which their husbands had to pay child support.

1,600 BC – War and peace

There followed a thousand years of war and peace. The Egyptians vied with the Babylonians and a new Mesopotamian power, the Assyrians, for territory and influence. War became part of the texture of life: a citizen of the great Egyptian city of Thebes 3,000 years ago could hardly have conceived of a world without some war or other against the Assyrians of Tiglath Pileser. Many of us lived under the shadow of US-Soviet rivalry for decades yet the Cold War lasted less than half a century; imagine it had lasted back to the Battle of Hastings in 1066 and you have some idea of how unchanging and unchangeable was the political world of a citizen of Thebes.

2,000 BC – Aryan invaders

If history has any consistent lesson it is that all civilizations decay – to be revitalized from outside by the vibrant force of a different set of people. Such change in the ancient world was always engendered by the 'barbarians'. In the Mediterranean the threat came from the Aryan peoples of Central Europe.

The forgotten Pharaohs

Most histories barely acknowledge that Egypt at its peak was conquered by a civilization from the African interior. The kingdom of Kush in what is now Sudan rose to prominence around 800 BC and seized power over Egypt. The Kushites ruled as Pharaohs for just over a hundred years before retreating to within their own borders. The Kushite civilization thrived for a thousand years until around AD 300. They were primarily stock breeders and cultivators but they had an impressive Egyptian-style capital at Meroe, a priest culture and they traded across the Red Sea. They were also one of the earliest peoples to develop an alphabetic script, one every bit as effective as the Greek. Their most notable export though was the training of elephants for war – Hannibal's epic crossing of the Alps to fight the Romans derived from Kushite knowledge. ∎

The word 'Aryan' was hijacked by Hitler to describe his ridiculous Nordic 'master race'. But Aryans were much more broadly based than this. Many of the great civilizations – the Greeks, the Persians, the Romans and the Vedic Hindus, for example – were all originally nomadic barbarians from Europe who first conquered and then adopted city life.

These Aryan people spread out widely. Like the Nazis they wanted 'living room', probably because their population was expanding too fast for a nomadic lifestyle to cope. They cultivated wheat but moved on in their ox-drawn carts after every harvest. So as the Aryan population grew it had to spread into new regions, by conquest if necessary.

One wave of invaders streamed into Britain and Ireland using their bronze weapons to subjugate the original inhabitants. This first wave, the Gaelic Celts, built the great stone monuments of Stonehenge and Avebury but were then pushed into Ireland and Scotland by a later wave of invaders with iron weapons. These were the Brythonic Celts, who were themselves driven back into Wales and Cornwall by further invaders.

2,000 BC – Origins of Hindu caste

Aryan peoples had also had an impact much further east in India. Around 2,000 BC the first Indian civilization died. No-one knows exactly why. The flooding of the Indus or an epidemic may have been to blame but equally their cities may have been destroyed by waves of horse-riding Aryan invaders. These are the invaders celebrated in the ancient Hindu texts, the Vedas, and their speech became the holy language of Sanskrit. From the first, these pale-colored Aryans seem to have refused to intermingle with the dark-skinned inhabitants of India, the Dravidians, and a rigid social hierarchy developed from this. In India today people of the higher castes still tend to have lighter skin than those of lower or no caste.

538 BC – The Persian Empire

Even the superpowers like Assyria suffered from Aryan expansion. Over a century Assyria was weakened more and more by barbarian attacks and eventually crumbled when faced by an unprecedented alliance of Semitic Chaldeans from the south and Aryan Persians from the north-east. Two great empires resulted from a division of the Assyrian spoils. The first was the new Chaldean empire of Babylonia which was to achieve its

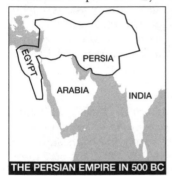

THE PERSIAN EMPIRE IN 500 BC

greatest heights of wealth and power under Nebuchadnezzar the Great. But even this was swallowed in 538 BC by the second great empire, that of the Persians.

The Persian Empire of Darius I was the greatest the world had yet seen and was bewilderingly vast even by today's standards, stretching from Egypt to India, and from Arabia to the Caspian Sea. It was only possible to administer all this because horses and chariots were now available for faster communications – and the Persians built the first made roads in the world.

1,000 BC – The first feudal system

The Chinese also had problems with barbarians – with the Mongolian steppe peoples who had first learned how to ride and control horses. But the Chinese took a significant step towards a unified China in the 11th century BC when the frontier state of Chou overcame the Shang to establish a new dynasty and subjugate peoples as far south as the Yangtze river. The Chou dynasty then imposed the first feudal state in the world, well over a thousand years before Europe evolved the same sorry social system. Supporters of the emperor were given fiefdoms, and they in turn offered land to their supporters, while the peasants at the bottom of the pyramid toiled to produce food and wealth to keep their lords in the style to which they were accustomed.

This feudal system survived intact even when the Chou empire succumbed to further invaders in 771 BC: China then sank into one of its periods of disunity, with over 100 local lords breaking away from the emperor to form their own small states. This would not necessarily have been bad for the peasants, except that each lord felt obliged to make war on his neighbor. Millions of ordinary people were dragooned into risking their lives. In the 500 years to 221 BC, the Chinese people had only 120 years of peace.

221 BC – The birth of China

Gradually, though, the shattered pieces of China began to reform. First the number of warring states shrank through conquest to seven and trade started to increase as a result. Finally, in 318 BC, the westernmost of the seven states, Ch'in, which had stayed out of previous conflicts and built up its strength, started to annex its neighbors. By 221 BC China had been unified and had assumed from Ch'in the name by which it is known today.

Prince Cheng, its able young ruler, declared himself Shih Huang-ti (first emperor) and launched a harsh regime which involved people in crippling amounts of military service and public work. Some of the work was useful: a national network of roads and canals, and the standardization of written Chinese.

The Great Wall was begun as a defense against predatory Mongolians, but was otherwise known as the longest cemetery in the world because it claimed so many laborers' lives. Indeed we generally remember ancient civilizations best by those buildings which most exploited the labor of ordinary people and most glorified the vanity of a single autocrat.

4 God and the spirit

Prophets and seers arise all over Asia in the sixth century BC, laying down the roots of most modern major religions.

THE SIXTH CENTURY BC was one of the most remarkable epochs in human history. Yet no political leader or historian of that age could possibly have guessed why people like us, 25 centuries on, would remember it. There may be a lesson in this – perhaps our own age will be remembered less for computers and air travel, nuclear weapons and Moon landings than for the birth of an obscure prophet whose ideas will sweep the world in the coming centuries. EF Schumacher, this is your life?

Confucius and Lao-tzu

China's national character was formed much less by emperors than by two altogether less warlike figures who lived in the sixth century BC: K'ung Fu-tzu (known in the West as Confucius) and Lao-tzu. The former lived as a noble in the small state of Lu, where he set up a kind of academy for discovering and teaching wisdom. His own wisdom was really an elaborate and rigid system of rules by which people might live in disciplined society. It was more a deeply conservative philosophy than a religion, and it was to become the cornerstone of the imperial hierarchy for over two thousand years. As might be expected, it did not carry a very exalted view of women's importance: of the five fundamental relationships which constituted natural harmony, only that of husband and wife involved women. K'ung Fu-tzu never found a sympathetic ruler but his ideas spread like wildfire across northern China after his death in 478 BC.

Southern China preferred the thinking of Lao-tzu, who was for a time chief librarian to the emperor, and whose advice was both more mystical and more elusive. The gist of his teaching was that life and nature form an indivisible whole, with every positive element having its equivalent negative aspect, every yang its yin. According to his belief, the earth and the universe regulate themselves according to certain eternal principles; this was the Tao or the Way, and the religion based on his work thus became known as Taoism. Campaigners for ecological concerns in the West in the last few years have noticed the similarity between their notion of the planet as a self-regulating ecosystem which humans have abused and the Taoist conception of life on earth.

Gautama Buddha

By 600 BC the Aryan people who dominated northern India had founded 16 separate city states on the Gangetic plain, continually at each other's throats. And into an influential family in one of these tiny states was born, around 563 BC, Siddhartha Gautama, who was to become the Buddha.

Gautama was born into great material comfort and by the time his life changed completely he was married with a baby son. He questioned why he was not happy and this led him to set out as a penniless seeker after spiritual truth. He tried all the established methods, including severe self-mortification, before finally achieving enlightenment in his own way and dedicating the rest of his life to teaching people what he had learned. The gist of this (the *Dhamma*) was that the root of unhappiness was selfish desire: all beings were reincarnated and struggled through the ages to learn how to liberate themselves from the passion and selfishness which kept them tied to the wheel of rebirth. This message did not achieve wide currency in his lifetime but was to spread far and wide in the centuries to come.

Its sophisticated understanding of human psychology was far beyond anything achieved in the world hitherto. Sadly it did not extend its benefits to all people equally. It was only with great reluctance that the Buddha allowed women to form a monastic order: he felt it would hold back the general progress towards spiritual liberation. And on his deathbed he is said to have confided his views on women to his disciple Ananda: 'Women are full of passion, Ananda; women are envious, Ananda; women are stupid, Ananda. That is the reason, Ananda, that is the cause, why women have no place in public assemblies, do not carry on business, and do not earn their living by any profession'.

The Hebrews and their Father God

The spiritual impact of the sixth century BC did not stop with Lao-tzu and the Buddha. Barely noticed by any contemporary observer would have been the Hebrews, whose history has an impact even today on the politics of the Middle East. The Hebrews were Semitic nomads who invaded Palestine from the east around 1,500 BC. They secured no more than a foothold against the Philistines and spent the next 500 years confined to the hill country around the River Jordan.

Until then the Hebrews had been ruled by priestly judges selected by the tribal elders. But around 1,000 BC they chose a king, Saul, to lead them into battle. And his successor, David, brought about the only prosperous period in Hebrew history. Even then this was due to the patronage of a more powerful Semitic ruler – King Hiram of the great Phoenician trading city of Tyre, who wanted a trade route through Hebrew country to the Red Sea. Trade expanded and the city of Jerusalem and its temple were built. David's son Solomon inherited this increasing prosperity and was rather intoxicated by his own magnificence, which in reality was extremely limited. At his death the country split into two: Israel in the north and Judea, based on Jerusalem, in the south.

Existence for both kingdoms became precarious,

sandwiched as they were between the superpowers Assyria and Babylon. In 722 BC Israel was conquered by Assyria and its people were swept into captivity or extinction. Judea struggled on until 587 BC when it suffered the same fate at the hands of Babylon. But this time the outcome was different. In Babylon the people of Judea, whom we can begin to call Jews, learned how to read and write and transcribed their history, hitherto handed down orally, in what was to become the Jewish Torah and the first books of the Christian Bible. It gave them a new sense of themselves, the kind of binding force and cultural cohesion which no people on earth had hitherto possessed. And when Babylon itself fell to the Persians in 538 BC, the Jews were allowed to return to Jerusalem imbued with this new sense of themselves as a nation, as the chosen people of a single omnipotent God.

As far as we know this was the first time that any people had advanced the idea of one all-powerful male god. It set the seal on the establishment of male rule in human society: in the new hierarchy of power the patriarchal God sat at the top, men were lords of creation, made in his image, and women were different and subservient afterthoughts.

There were further implications. In other religious systems you might choose your favorite deity from among many. But with Judaism's belief in One God – and the Christianity and Islam which were to follow – came the idea of religious orthodoxy and the duty to convert, persecute or wage war in his name. The flip side of that coin is that Judaism provided for the first time a moral reference point which would help people to rebel against their rulers on the grounds of individual conscience. Besides, the new idea was appealing for its revolutionary simplicity. It was particularly appealing to the Jews since it made them a special race, God's chosen people. At a time when the once-powerful Semitic peoples were being conquered all over the Mediterranean world, this doctrine was

The greatest king in history

The Buddha's sense that life was full of misery may well have been fostered by the continual warring of the states of northern India. His monasteries must have seemed islands of sanity in a fevered era of pointless power-seeking and conflict. It is ironic then that Buddhism became a world religion because one of those city states was successful enough to conquer all the others and unify most of India under its rule.

This was Magadha, nucleus of the great empire founded in 322 BC by Chandragupta Maurya. Chandragupta is said to have visited Alexander the Great in an unsuccessful attempt to persuade him to conquer all India. In the end he did much of the job himself and in addition drove the Greeks out of the Indus region. Chandragupta's son extended the empire further and his grandson Asoka, when he succeeded to the throne in 264 BC, was initially inclined to finish the task and push on southward beyond Madras to conquer the whole subcontinent. But instead his first conquest left him so disgusted by the pain and suffering it caused that – in a gesture which for a conqueror is utterly unique – he renounced warfare completely. He converted to Buddhism and vowed that henceforth his conquests would be spiritual. To that end he sent out missionaries to Ceylon, Siam and Burma; eventually these bore fruit in the Buddhism which all three countries retain to this day.

But Asoka also put his principles into practice as a temporal ruler. His 28-year reign saw all the energy which had previously gone into pointless warfare channelled into constructive work. He encouraged women's education. Wells were dug all over the country, trees planted and hospitals built. He created a ministry for the care of the indigenous peoples of the country, an amazingly modern concept which the modern Government of India has still not fully taken on board. But after his death the impetus slackened and India descended again into a period of division during which the Hindu Brahmins successfully fought off the Buddhist challenge. Still, Asoka deserves to be remembered as perhaps the most enlightened monarch in world history. ■

bound to have a magnetic force. And over the next few hundred years, as Semitic civilizations were being destroyed as far apart as Spain and Carthage, communities of 'Jews' sprang up in the same places. These dislocated Semitic peoples had similar origins, appearances and languages to the Hebrews. It is not surprising that they cleaved to an idea that elevated them above even their conquerors.

5 Greek and Latin

The Greeks lay down the foundations for modern science and practise a democracy our own leaders would call impossibly idealistic. Alexander the Great spreads their ideas when he conquers half the world. The baton is then taken up by the Romans who make one addition we could well have managed without – slave plantations.

THE GREEKS WERE an Aryan group who destroyed the original Aegean civilizations such as Troy and Crete and eventually established separate city states like Athens, Sparta and Corinth. These cities often fought amongst themselves – but came together once every four years for the great Olympic athletic competitions. The Greeks' epic versions of their early history – the *Iliad* and the *Odyssey* – could only be written down in the seventh century BC once they had learned about writing from the Phoenicians. The epic tales gave Greeks a common heritage and helped bind their city states together.

507 BC – The first democracy

Athens was the greatest of these city states. And for once greatness was measured not by prowess in war (at which the Spartans were possibly better) but by intellectual and political development. In 507 BC the Athenian leader Cleisthenes 'took the people into partnership'. And from this evolved the notion of democracy (government by *demos*, the people) which the Greeks handed down to the world.

There were some pretty basic flaws to this version of democracy: women took no part, had no rights and were even prohibited from leaving their houses at night. Beneath the women were the slaves, probably descendants of the original Aegeans, whose labor helped make the achievements of Greek civilization possible.

But even so, Athenian democracy had plenty to teach us. All citizens could speak and vote in the Assembly – and if all the 65,000 men who qualified in the Athens of 431 BC actually turned up it would have been a pretty difficult meeting to chair. Day-to-day problems were dealt with by an executive council of 50 men which served for a tenth of a year and was chosen by lot. Anyone who looked to have too much ambition would be voted down.

Many prehistoric peoples would have worked through consensus. But Athens was the first state to put a premium on the involvement of the majority, if only of men, in the political process. One of its greatest statespeople, Pericles, said: 'We do not call a man who does not share in public life politically quietist; we call him politically useless', a sentiment which could not be endorsed with genuine conviction by many rulers in the 21st century.

400 BC – Art and science

The Greeks didn't break new ground in politics alone. Art was encouraged and great dramas were produced by the likes of Aeschylus, Sophocles and Euripides. But the main advance was in intellectual thought and debate. Unlike previous civilizations, within which priests had held a virtual monopoly on learning, academic research was widely valued in Athenian society. The value of open-minded discussion and logical argument was discovered by people like Socrates. His pupil Plato taught political philosophy and drew up a vision of an ideal society, his *Republic*: the first appearance of the idea that humans could create a better world out of their own will and imagination.

Plato's pupil Aristotle chose a different road – that of scientific inquiry. He believed that people had to assemble as much knowledge as possible before they could progress. Unfortunately Aristotle also handed down perhaps the most systematic and rigid ideas about gender yet put into words: 'The male shapes and molds society and the world. Woman, on the other hand, is passive. She stays at home, as is her nature. She is matter waiting to be formed by the active male principle.' You would not have guessed from this that prominent women thinkers abounded in Athens: to give just one example, both Socrates and Plato were taught by Aspatia of Miletos.

338 BC – Alexander the Great

The Greeks may have led the world in philosophy but they did not become a military superpower until their contending city states were united in 338 BC – conquered by Philip, king of Macedonia. Philip's dream was for Greeks to take over the Persian Empire. He was assassinated before he could launch an invasion but his son Alexander, who had been educated by Aristotle, then took up the challenge. He invaded Asia Minor and launched upon an 11-year campaign of fantastic military success which not only conquered the Persian Empire but also peoples as far apart as Egypt and northwest India. He died of fever in 323 BC at the age of just 32, having led his army over 11,000 miles (17,600 kilometers). His empire then fell apart but the export of Greek culture and encouragement of trade continued for centuries because the lands were divided between three of his Macedonian generals.

Ptolemy was one of these generals and he set up his own dynasty of Pharaohs in Egypt. This eventually became as moribund and stagnant as any other hereditary institution but the heritage of Aristotle was carried a little further. A great library was established in the new city of Alexandria, together with a museum which financed and encouraged the work of all the great scientific minds of the day. But all this intellectual work was sealed off from the ordinary people who might have been able to use and develop it. Everything remained abstract and, in the absence of paper, ideas moldered on the dusty shelves of the élite.

272 BC – The rise of Rome

The Romans inherited the western portion of Alexander's empire. Rome began as a small trading city but in the century up to 275 BC its people con-

AFRICA

THE ROMAN EMPIRE IN AD 50

quered the whole of Italy in a mood of expansionist self-confidence. This brought them into confrontation with Carthage, the Phoenician city across the Mediterranean which was then probably the greatest in the world. The 'Punic Wars' between these two new superpowers lasted on and off for over a hundred years, at which point, in 146 BC, the Romans destroyed Carthage, massacred 200,000 of its inhabitants and sold the remaining 50,000 into slavery. This left them in control of North Africa and Spain.

With the Carthaginians eliminated, the Romans turned their attention to Europe – and with a sense of civilizing mission previously absent from imperial conquest. Rome's soldiers and administrators imposed their own notions and culture on Europe – especially on lands they considered 'barbarian'. And as a result the modern French, Spanish, Italian, Portuguese and Romanian languages are all variations on a theme of Latin.

250 BC – Class struggle in Rome

Meanwhile the character of Rome itself was being changed by what we might, after Marx, call class struggle. The common people (the plebeians) had battled for centuries with the aristocracy (the patricians) for the right to a say in government. By the fourth century BC their battle had to some extent been won: plebeian men had full rights of citizenship. There were still noble families but the gap between rich and poor had not yet become alarming.

It was the Empire which changed things. Until the First Punic War, Rome had been a community of free farmers but many of these were conscripted for military service overseas and their farms fell into debt. Slaves supplied the food deficit, either by being shipped in to work the Roman estates or by working on large-scale slave farms in new colonies such as Sicily. The ordinary Roman citizens returned from military service to find that they were now the poor, in hock to a new breed of aristocratic wealth based on the ownership of slaves. They had also been disenfranchised since most power was now exercised through the Senate – effectively a debating chamber of patricians – rather than through the Popular Assembly in which anyone and everyone male (as in Athens) could vote.

History books have relatively little to say about this internal political struggle between rich and poor. We generally hear more about the 'great men' of the patrician families. But in the second and first centuries BC there was a series of revolutionary upheavals. They were attempts to seize back the large farming estates from the rich and abolish the debts which held the poor in check. They failed. So too did the slaves who revolted under Spartacus in 73 BC and held off the Roman army for two years before they were defeated: 6,000 of them were crucified along the road to Rome.

49 BC – Caesar's military coup

With the defeat of the common Roman came the destruction of the republican spirit. The army grew into a full-time paid force and the political power which its patrician commander wielded grew with it. Two of these commanders, Marius and later Julius Caesar, secured their position ruthlessly by murdering opponents. Caesar refused the title of 'king' when he became dictator but after visiting Cleopatra in Egypt (a descendant of Alexander's general Ptolemy) returned with notions of himself as an 'Unconquerable God' that eventually led to his assassination. His nephew Octavian had no such delusions but made himself the first emperor with the name Augustus Caesar (thus bequeathing an exalted title to future monarchs and dictators – the Iranian Shah, the German Kaiser and the Russian Czar are all versions of Caesar).

The Roman emperors varied in ability and in sanity but gave to a larger area of the globe a longer period of relative peace than it has experienced in the rest of recorded history. They must have thought their civilization eternal – yet it carried the seeds of its own destruction from the moment ordinary citizens at home and in the colonies were put down and a slave culture was established. From then on an élite was catered for by vast numbers of slaves in the food-producing fields, in the home and in the gladiatorial arena. These slaves (especially in the earlier centuries) were brutally treated, not allowed to marry or own property, and could legally be mutilated or killed at the will of their owners. Both young boys and women were routinely abused sexually by the male Roman élite. In the Roman household the father had the power of life and death over women and children and was the only full person in the eyes of the law. And even 'free' peasants in the colonized lands had a harsh and overtaxed time – the standard rate of tax in North Africa was one-third of the harvest plus six days' labor.

AD 350 – The Empire implodes
The mass of people received little benefit from the Roman Empire. So when the 'barbarian hordes' – the Franks, Vandals and Visigoths from Central Europe – began to break through in the third and fourth centuries AD, they must have been seen by many as liberators.

Besides, the Empire was already decaying. Once it

stopped expanding and there was no more booty to add to the bank balance, the economic costs of maintaining such a large empire came home to roost. The upper classes spent all their money on Indian, Chinese and Arabian luxury goods. That helped to undermine the value of the Roman currency, with the result that hyper-inflation took hold: a measure of

The end of the Roman Empire

From around AD 235, 'barbarians', including Huns and Visigoths, attacked the Empire and set up kingdoms in Britain, France and Germany. As it weakened and Christianity spread, in AD 395 the Roman empire was divided into West and East; the Eastern capital was Byzantium (Constantinople). By the end of the fifth century power in Rome and Byzantium was in the hands of 'barbarian' warlords. ■

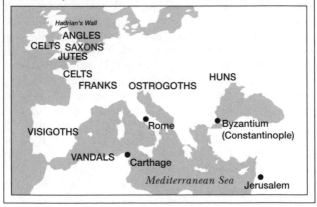

wheat which cost 200 drachmae in the Roman Egypt of AD 276 cost 3,000 in 314, 78,000 in 334 and 2,000,000 not long after that. Perhaps this is how the decline and fall of the Western Empire will be marked, too – not with a nuclear bang but with the whimper of imploding dollars.

6 The rise and rise of religion

Two even more powerful claimants to the ear of the Father God emerge: Jesus and Muhammad. From the most unpromising beginnings they offer such inspiration that they become the guiding force of empires and the guiding light of inner lives right into our own time.

ROME HAD LOST its sense of civilizing mission by the end. It had no ideas left to export. But with almost its dying breath it bequeathed to the world something it had spent centuries rejecting and suppressing.

During the rule of Augustus Caesar a boy called Jesus was born in the subject Roman province of Judea. Little is known of his early life but at about the age of 30 he began to attract attention and followers as a religious prophet. He spoke, like Isaiah and the other Jewish prophets before him, of one God to whom all would answer. But while he preached almost entirely to Jews, he did not single them out: this was a God for all people of all races. The prophet Isaiah had already refined the raging desert god of the Hebrews into a universal deity who urged people to challenge injustice and care for the poor; the compassionate and merciful God which Jesus spoke of was a development of this. Not surprisingly many Jews were threatened and offended by this apparent hijacking of their creed. And the authorities, both Jewish and Roman, found Jesus' new social and political teachings treasonable, since they were revolutionary in their unequivocal egalitarianism. After three years of preaching, Jesus was executed as a subversive.

AD 50 – The early Church
Jesus' later life and teachings are described in the four 'gospels' of the Christian New Testament. But the Church he inspired was instructed too by the writings of the early Christians – particularly those of St Paul,

who enshrined the idea that Jesus had sacrificed himself (and been resurrected) to bring humanity the chance of eternal life. He also enshrined the patriarchal attitudes of the Church and accepted the institution of slavery, which seems distinctly at odds with the revolutionary value Jesus had put upon every individual.

Like any prophet, Jesus' message was transmuted by the perceptions and enthusiasms of his followers. Gautama Buddha was absolutely clear that he, himself, was not a god but simply a teacher. Yet Buddhists have for centuries worshipped his image and prayed for his blessing on their lives. So too once Christ was dead the battle began over his meaning. Early Christians were bitterly at odds over whether Jesus was separate from and inferior to God; whether he was God; or whether God was made up not only of himself and Jesus but also a third force, the Holy Spirit. The last of these ideas, the Holy Trinity, won the day. And, as with any other ideological orthodoxy, once it was accepted by the Church establishment, those who disagreed with it were considered beyond the pale, not true Christians, even if they believed in every word that Jesus spoke in the Gospels.

Early Christianity also adopted aspects of other religions popular at the time such as Alexandrianism (with its notion of three aspects of one god) and Mithraism (which had the age-old idea that blood sacrifice brought about rebirth) – it absorbed their altars and temples, their candles and chanting. This made its acceptance by new converts much easier, though its moral force, its fervent belief in the value of all people, must also have been powerfully attractive in an age so dominated by human bondage.

324 – A Christian empire
The word spread through the first two centuries after Christ's death, despite numerous attempts by Roman emperors to stamp out this dangerous new cult,

culminating in a great persecution ordered by the Emperor Diocletian in 303 which saw Church property confiscated, religious writings destroyed and many Christians executed. The viciousness of this persecution – and the quiet courage with which many Christian adherents faced it – may ironically have contributed towards a dramatic reversal. The next emperor, Galerius, issued an edict of toleration and in 312 his successor Constantine abandoned any divine pretensions and instead put Christian symbols on the shields and banners of his troops. From 324 onwards Christianity was the official religion of the Empire and its place as a dominant force in the world was secured.

450 – From Attila to the Pope

The decline of Rome allowed local peoples to regain their influence in Europe, each in their different way. In what is now France the Gauls would often take over a town and simply run it in the Romans' stead, settling, intermarrying and learning Latin. In England three German groups, the Angles, Saxons and Jutes, pursued a quite different strategy. They invaded towards the end of the fourth century and in a policy similar to that adopted by the Khmer Rouge in modern Cambodia they destroyed the Roman towns (as farmers they had no use for these) and used their own languages, which became English. The Huns had a style all of their own. They were a nomadic

The African Christians

Christianity reached the African interior very early on. The Queen of Kush had an ambassador in Jerusalem who was preached to by Christ's apostle Philip as they traveled together to Gaza in the Kushite's chariot.

Nobody knows whether this Kushite official spread the word at home. The first Christian country in sub-Saharan Africa we are sure about was Axum in the Tigray region of modern Ethiopia. This was a powerful trading kingdom which had emerged by the first century AD. By the fourth century its Red Sea trade was prosperous enough for gold coins to be issued – and these bore a cross. The religion of Ethiopia has been Christian ever since. ∎

Mongolian group who had probably been pushed west by a climatic change in Central Asia. They rampaged through Gaul, the Balkans and Italy before disappearing from view after the death of their leader Attila. By the end of the fifth century, Rome itself had been sacked twice and power there – as well as in the capital of the Eastern Empire, Constantinople – was in the hands of 'barbarian' warlords.

Europe was still nominally subject to the authority of Rome, though this meant next to nothing in practice. In 476 Odoacer, leader of a confederation of German groups, announced that there would no longer be an emperor in Rome and power passed instead to the Patriarch of Rome or 'Pope', who made himself head of the Church in the emperor's stead. But the Greek-speaking eastern half of the empire was by now an independent entity with its own emperor based in Constantinople – relic of a dispute between two sons of an emperor over the succession.

This eastern or Byzantine empire showed a bit more life, particularly under Justinian I and his equally able wife Theodora. But in religious terms it was possessed by the notion of Orthodoxy; the words of a distinctly free thinker, Jesus, had by now been codified into a remarkably rigid system of beliefs. And the energy of the Byzantine empire was dissipated by futile and apparently endless warring with its eastern neighbor, Persia, over both land and religion. The Persian kings had resurrected the ancient local religion of Zoroastrianism and persecuted any Christian infiltration. The Byzantine-Persian wars are both depressing and tedious to contemplate even from this distance. They must have been more than depressing for the inhabitants of Egypt and Asia Minor, whose lands were caught in between and kept in a state of devastation as a result.

But this already-decadent religious world was about to be put to the flaming sword of Islam.

570 – The vision of Muhammad

Islam was the last of the great world religions to emerge. It derives from the teaching of Muhammad ibn Abdullah, who was born in 570 in Mecca, a small town in the Arabian desert. Until he was 40 Muhammad did little of note but marry the widow of a rich merchant. But then he began to have prophetic visions. He declared himself the Prophet of the one God, the last in a line that included Abraham, Moses and Jesus. Mecca was the home of the pagan shrine of the Black Stone, the Ka'bah, which contained some 360 sacred stones and statues. Pilgrims came to it from all over Arabia. So when Muhammad started to preach against it the locals attacked him and he had to escape to Medina, 180 miles (290 kilometers) away. People there were more receptive to his message.

Medina became the first Muslim state. The first mosque was built and it was from Medina that Muhammad gathered an army of 10,000 and led an attack on Mecca. The city surrendered and the idols in the Ka'bah were smashed. But Muhammad cannily retained the Black Stone itself as the prime site of Muslim pilgrimage, which it remains to this day.

Islam, like Christianity, absorbed the traditions of preceding religions. It encompassed not just Judaism (southern Arabia at the time was mainly Jewish) and Christianity but also the local pagan worship, including the ancient religion of the Great Goddess.

The coming of Islam could not be said to have improved the lot of local women. In pre-Islamic Arabia a woman had the right to choose her own husbands and practise polyandry; when she was pregnant she simply chose which husband was to be the father. Muhammad reversed this to give men sexual power and the right to practise polygamy. As with Jesus, though, Muhammad's own thoughts on women as recorded in the Qur'an were much less negative than those of the followers who helped shape the religion. The early Muslim sage Ghazali, for example, claimed that men had 999 of the components of merit and women only one.

632 – Holy War

Muhammad spent the last part of his life converting the rest of Arabia to Islam by military force. After his death in 632 his followers took up the flame and set about conquering the world in the name of Allah. It was a completely crazy idea – the Arab army numbered at first no more than a few thousand. But the capacity of Islam to inspire those who came into contact with it made them a mighty military power.

They smashed the Byzantine army in 636 and soon took over the tired countries of Egypt and Asia Minor. Their new religious idea must have been grasped enthusiastically by people who had been squeezed between the oppressive rectitude of Byzantine Christianity and mystic Zoroastrianism. Here was a faith that was utterly simple. There were no priests or temples to act as barriers between the human and the divine, just a faith in the one true God before whom all races and classes were equal.

Islam's simple, fervent message carried all before it in a series of conquests more remarkable than those of Alexander, Attila or the Caesars. Within a century of Muhammad's death, the Muslims had conquered Persia, Afghanistan and Turkestan to take them as far east as the Chinese border. In the west they had overcome Africa north of the Sahara, Spain and even half of France until they were pushed back to the Pyrenees in 732.

661 – Sunnis and Shi'a

There were, however, to be branches of Islam. You may be confused today by the breach between the Sunni Islam favored by Saudi Arabia and the Shi'a version adhered to by Iran. This split occurred as early as 661. The Umayyad family were recognized as Caliphs (heads of Islam) over the competing claim of the

Islamic technology

The initial wave of Muslim invaders thought the Qur'an (Koran) the only book that mattered. So they started to destroy all the others; they even burned the Great Library at Alexandria. But they soon changed their minds. As they came into contact with ideas from China and India, Muslims launched themselves into the pursuit of knowledge.

Baghdad was established as a brand new capital and became the cultural center of the world. Islamic scholars studied the Greek classics at a time when Europe had forgotten them. They also gathered new mathematical ideas from India and spread them throughout their empire – algebra is an Arabic word. They learned from the Chinese how to make paper and started printing.

But they also made great advances of their own in both medical and physical science. The discovery that blood circulates throughout the body is traditionally attributed to the 17th-century British scientist William Harvey. Yet Muslims knew about this long before. And their alchemists introduced the systematic approach that we now know as 'scientific method'. Universities sprang up all over the Arab world in the eighth and ninth centuries – though for the benefit only of men, a precedent that is too often still followed today.

The Christian monks who kept the light of learning alive in Dark Ages Europe were mostly just copying ancient texts rather than making progress of their own. But the Arabs took similar raw material and turned it into something new and exciting – and kept the world's intellectual wheels revolving. Islam was to be the leading civilization of the western hemisphere for a thousand years after the birth of Muhammad.

It even spawned a financial system. A full banking service grew up to finance trade and industry throughout the vast Muslim empire – it became possible to take out a bank draft in Mecca and cash it in Marrakech. There may be times when we would not thank them for inventing it, but we owe our modern banking system to the early Muslims. ∎

Prophet's own cousin and son-in-law. Those who accepted this succession became the Sunnis. Those who opposed it became the Shi'a.

Despite these divisions, such is the religion's cultural and spiritual power that, from Afghanistan to Morocco, almost all the countries which were conquered in the blazing first century have remained Muslim to this day.

7 Light in the East

Europe descends into a feudal Dark Ages. Indians, meanwhile, are discovering mathematics. And China is ever shaping and shattering – but is still the most cultured country in the world.

AFTER THE ROMAN empire fell apart, 'barbarian' peoples in Europe – most of them Christian converts – settled down into a new social structure similar to the feudalism of China. This was built on the power of warlords who built castles to keep themselves secure and called themselves kings or dukes. Peasants worked the land but also had to serve their lord in battle and keep him in relative luxury in return for his 'protection'. Europe was atomized into thousands of petty provinces. Roads fell into disrepair since travel and trade no longer seemed important.

This was the 'Dark Ages': Europe lost whatever light had been cast on art, science and philosophy by the ancient Mediterranean civilizations. The light was kept alive only by priests, nuns and monks. They were virtually the only people who saw a value in learning and were considered inviolate by even the pettiest local tyrant.

But there were great developments elsewhere in the world. Had the Chinese traveled as far as Europe in, say, the seventh century, they would have been unimpressed. And if in later centuries they had been ruthless enough to back this sense of superiority with the gunpowder they had invented, the world might be very different today.

Many Westerners have trouble getting to grips with China. The names are unfamiliar – apart from Ming vases, perhaps, or 'Confucius he say'. A truly internationalist history of the world has to respect what has always been the world's most populous country. Yet because we have few reference points there's a danger that we'll switch off when confronted by a long list of emperors and dynasties, warlords and barbarian invasions.

AD 23 – Chinese patterns

Chinese history is certainly repetitious: the same patterns crop up again and again. A new imperial dynasty will take over and dominate a relatively united China, as the Han did for the four centuries that spanned the birth of Christ. The dynasty is always threatened by invasion from the nomadic peoples of the steppes beyond the Great Wall. Just as often, though, they will be deposed by revolution – peasant revolts occur more often in the history of China than of any other region. It is a Western myth that the 'fatalistic' Oriental temperament led its people to submit to the will of destiny and a strict imperial hierarchy.

The peasant rebellions which brought down the Han dynasty were partly prompted by a terrible plague which swept the ancient world in the second century. But they were mainly provoked by excessive taxation. Such rebellions often resulted in full-blown civil wars like the one sparked by the Revolt of the Yellow Turbans in 184 which sprawled over three decades. This makes the English Civil War (1642-1649), for example, look like a minor disturbance.

220 – The great kaleidoscope

According to the Chinese pattern, after a dynasty is deposed there ensues a period of chaos in which there is no centralized control and local warlords vie with each other for power and influence in a vast jigsaw of mini-states. Such decentralization might not seem so terrible but in fact all the great developments in Chinese history, whether material or cultural, occurred during the eras of strict imperial control rather than those of local autonomy. So in the time after the fall of the Han, which is known as The Age of

Confusion, much of the north seems to have reverted to a barter economy.

Chinese history is like a great kaleidoscope, endlessly forming and fragmenting, forming and fragmenting. The next unification of China occurred under some Turko-Chinese aristocrats from the northwest, the Sui, who were the first emperors to adopt the ideas of K'ung Fu-tzu. These 'Confucian' principles in education and the civil service were to be followed right into the 20th century. They also set about the construction of a great canal system to link the agriculture of the south with the armies and administrative centers of the north. Some of these are still in use. But the Sui showed less wisdom in attempting costly conquests of outlying regions like Annam and Kokurea (modern Vietnam and Korea). The wars themselves were disastrous but the taxation and conscription they involved were even more so – there was a rash of popular revolts throughout China which in 618 resulted in the assassination of the emperor Yang-ti.

626 – The most civilized country

The new imperial dynasty was the T'ang, which during the reign of the emperor Tai-tsung transformed China into the most advanced and civilized country in the world. Its capital, Changan, was by far the largest city anywhere, with a million people within its walls by the eighth century – London and Paris did not reach this size for another 1,100 years. Changan was a cosmopolitan place, full of Indian, Turkish and Japanese visitors. Buddhism caused a religious and philosophical revival; new schools of literature and poetry burgeoned to produce work of great beauty. Paper had already been in use in China for five centuries but now texts started to be printed with wood-blocks: the oldest surviving printed book in the world is a Buddhist text in Chinese, the Diamond Sutra.

China's dynasties

1,700 BC The first Chinese civilization is ruled by the Shang.

1,000 BC The Shang dynasty is conquered by Chou nomads, who establish the first feudal system.

771 BC Chou dynasty is overthrown.

221 BC China is united by the first emperor, Shih Huang-ti. The Great Wall is soon begun.

202 BC The Han dynasty is established.

AD 23 The capital Changan is sacked by nomadic invaders.

220 Han dynasty falls.

626 The T'ang dynasty, under the emperor Tai-tsung, revives art and religion.

907 T'ang dynasty falls. Rise of the Sung dynasty in the south.

1368 Chu Yuan-chang becomes the first Ming emperor.

1644 Suicide of last Ming emperor as rebels take Peking. Manchu Ch'ing/Qing dynasty established. ∎

Above all there was a spirit of inquiry which had been absent from the world since the heyday of Athens. Christian and Muslim missionaries who arrived at the court of Tai-tsung were courteously received. Their religions were pronounced interesting and they were allowed to build a church and a mosque. The Chinese would hardly have met with such tolerance in a strange court in Europe.

907 – Political acts of God

The T'ang dynasty survived for almost three centuries. In military terms it was threatened by Islamic forces and also by Tibetans, who expanded to within a hundred miles of the Chinese capital in the eighth century – something worth remembering when we consider modern claims from Beijing that Tibet has always been part of China. In the end, though, the T'ang crumbled as a result of internal revolts rather than invasions. In the last part of the ninth century China suffered a series of terrible epidemics, floods and famines.

Even now the poorest people always suffer most from any natural disaster – the rich never starve even amidst the most terrible famine. Throughout history

Chinese peasants seem to have understood this basic political fact better than anyone else and have rebelled against their rulers in such circumstances: this is why a terrible natural disaster has always been said in China to herald the death of a dynasty.

The fall of the T'ang in 907 gave the kaleidoscope yet another turn and the northern half of the country fell into chaos. But in the south an impressive new civilization emerged under the Sung dynasty. There were major advances in agricultural technology – a kind of early Green Revolution with irrigation networks feeding new, more productive strains of rice. This was prompted by (and also encouraged) a spurt of population growth – China's population almost doubled in the three centuries to 1100, reaching 110 million. Trade and industry became more important and merchants acquired greater status. And as Confucian ideas took a tighter hold, people were recruited for the civil service on the basis of ability rather than family connections. Sung China was very largely a meritocracy as well as the richest, best-governed and most cultured country in the world.

320 – India gives the world zero

India was also going through a period of enlightenment during Europe's Dark Ages. After the collapse of Asoka's empire the subcontinent had splintered into numerous separate kingdoms. But much of the north was reunified from about 320 by the Gupta dynasty, which expanded by conquest from Asoka's old capital of Patna. Their most prominent king even took the name of an illustrious predecessor, though significantly this was the name of the warlike Chandragupta rather than the peace-making Asoka. He ruled over a country stretching from the Indus to the Bay of Bengal.

The Gupta success in war produced not more warfare but rather a period of great peace and prosperity – in this case the means certainly did not determine the end. India developed a major literature written in Sanskrit, including the definitive versions of the *Mahabharata* and the *Ramayana,* epic stories so powerful that they were to become the classical literature of the whole of southeast Asia. You will find these Hindu stories acted, danced, sung and retold today in Buddhist Thailand and Muslim Indonesia.

But the Guptas also bequeathed us something which we all use every day. They dreamed up the decimal numerical system and the invaluable concept of zero. They also invented the simple method of writing numbers still used worldwide today. These achievements have traditionally been attributed to the Arabs – simply because they passed them on to Europeans. But they were entirely Indian inventions, and as important to human development as literacy, say, or the wheel.

The Gupta state was undermined by continual Hunnish invasions and eventually fell in the middle of the sixth century. India lapsed yet again into disunity, into a tangle of warring states which was to last for more than 500 years. Some of these states were run by the Huns, though they soon became thoroughly Indianized: the Rajputs of modern northeast India are their direct descendants.

8 Wars of the cross

Christianity takes the center of the political stage. Popes maneuver, ordinary people take up arms in defense of their faith, monarchs put earthly power above heavenly rewards. And the European continent gets ready to plunder the rest of the planet.

THE FEUDAL SYSTEM in Europe was now highly developed – with a set of hierarchies rather like the management of a transnational corporation today. Originally it was just a relationship between a local warlord and his vassals. But now each lord (for ladies had little significance) had an overlord to pay tribute to; that overlord in turn had someone offering him protection; and so on up to the most powerful warlord of all, a duke or king.

Ordinary men and women remained largely unaffected by political machinations. Men worked their fields giving their lord a tax of part of their crops as well as occasionally doing military service for him. Women worked in the fields, did the domestic chores such as fetching water, grinding grains to make flour, preparing food and caring for children – and were taught every week at church about their inferiority to men in the eyes of God. Women's new position in Christian culture had become institutionalized: they had no rights to property or inheritance; they were 'given' by a father to a husband and had no right of divorce.

These people would have had little idea who was right at the top of the feudal social pyramid. But in fact by the eighth century most Europeans had a single overlord. Charles Martel was ruler of the Frankish kingdom which covered what is now France, Belgium and Holland. And when the Arab armies tried to expand their empire beyond Spain it was his forces which turned them back. His son extended Frankish influence over the German-speaking lands to

Europe takes shape

By the time Charlemagne died in 814, the nations of Europe were beginning to assume a recognizable shape. There were two main peoples within the Holy Roman Empire, those speaking the Frankish Latin dialect which was turning into French and those speaking various forms of German. The rivalry between these two was to continue deep into the 20th century.

In the east were Slavic groups, Bulgars and Poles, who were settling down in the countries that bear their names today. The Finns, Swedes, Norse and Danes in Scandinavia, meanwhile, retained their own traditions, largely outside the Christian orbit. Another of the Northern peoples – the Rus – pushed east to Kiev and had the largest country of all named after them. Others sailed across the Atlantic to set foot in North America five or six centuries before Columbus. And still more 'Norsemen' harried the coastline of western Europe. They battled their way to control of half the England of Alfred the Great in 886, while another group occupied the north of France in 912 and had it named after themselves as Normandy.

The conquest of England was completed in 1016 by Knut (the Canute of the English history books), who was simultaneously king of Norway and Denmark. Finally in 1066 the Normans crossed the Channel to England. They grafted their recently acquired French speech on to the English language. To this day many words considered upper-class in England are of French origin because for centuries the French-speaking Norman conquerors formed an aristocracy ruling over the Anglo-Saxon peasantry. ■

the east and his grandson, Charlemagne, thus inherited in 768 what was effectively a federated kingdom of Europe. He went on to conquer Rome and was crowned by the Pope - effectively the first of what came to be known as the Holy Roman Emperors.

1054 – Christian squabbles

The Holy Roman Emperor (whichever king had currently bludgeoned his way to the title) was generally at odds with the Pope – a rivalry which was to go on for centuries. And beyond these political squabbles there was also a religious one between the Catholic Church in Rome and the Greek Orthodox Church in Constantinople, which led ultimately to a divorce between these two Christian worlds in 1054.

Such petty European disputes and plots might seem

trivial against the whole tapestry of world history. But the Pope was by now the most important figure in Europe. He could challenge the authority of kings and emperors from his power base of monks and priests in every country. And he could also appeal to ordinary people directly. The Christian God was now having the same effect in Europe as Buddhism had throughout East Asia, and Islam through West Asia and North Africa. It was enabling humans to respond to an idea in a way that transcended local and group concerns.

1095 – The Pope's brainwave
This same effect was evident in the 11th century as Islam was revived by waves of invaders from the plains of Central Asia. These Turkish peoples conquered the Muslim Caliphate in Baghdad in the 10th century. But since they were recent converts to Islam, as fervent as the first holy warriors, the power of the Muslim faith was actually renewed. The pattern was repeated by a second group of Turks who established themselves in Baghdad in 1055 and called their leader 'sultan'. They took control of Palestine and threatened the Emperor

The Black Death
The most terrifying force in 14th century Europe was not a conquering army, but Death itself, in the shape of famine and plague. Between 1315 and 1319 there was widespread famine as a series of bad harvests came after an extremely rapid growth in population, especially in the cities. In the next three decades hunger became a regular problem for the poor in the cities – as in modern famines, the wealthier people had no trouble getting hold of food even in times of severe shortage. It became a regular feature of life for ordinary Europeans and was only banished by an even more terrible specter – the Black Death.

This epidemic of bubonic plague began in Asia and killed millions right across the known world between 1347 and 1353. Unlike famine, this killed both rich and poor alike, though given that it was carried by house rats, it attacked city dwellers more than country people. By the time it abated, some contemporary estimates put the death toll at one-third of the entire population of Europe: certainly many millions died and this made sudden, virtually inexplicable death a feared presence in everyone's life. ■

in Constantinople, who wrote in desperation to his estranged ally in Rome, the Pope.

At this point the Pope, Urban II, had a brainwave. European society was currently plagued by petty conflicts between small warlords and their conscripted peasant armies. When the Emperor's distress signal arrived Urban saw a way to absorb all this energy and re-establish his supremacy over Constantinople. He called for a truce in all wars between Christians and in 1095 declared a 'War of the Cross' or Crusade aimed at recapturing Jerusalem from the offending hands of the Turks.

1100 – The first propaganda

Propaganda was used to build up war fever – probably for the first time in history. The Pope's messengers spread outlandish stories about Turkish atrocities through France and Germany and produced a wave of popular outrage. In the 21st century we might hope to be more skeptical about such information. But in the 11th century people had no reason to distrust the news. They did not wait for formal armies but instead set out in large crowds to walk to the Holy Land and reclaim the Holy Sepulcher from the 'infidel'.

This was a remarkable phenomenon, showing just how deeply Christianity had embedded itself in the lives of ordinary people. It was perhaps the first real 'internationalist' movement. But it had disastrous results. Five large groups wandered off through Europe. Two went through Hungary, where they started killing Magyars on the grounds that they looked different and so must be pagans (in fact they had recently converted to Christianity). The Magyars took their revenge by massacring both groups. A third group later met the same end, though not before slaughtering Jewish communities in the Rhineland. The two remaining groups actually reached Constantinople, only to be annihilated by Turkish troops.

When the real 'First Crusade' took place it was

much more professional and led by Normans. After a two-year campaign they captured Jerusalem amid scenes of terrible slaughter. They held it for almost a century before the city fell to Muslims again. There were more crusades, including one from the Christian kingdom of Nubia in modern Sudan which was so badly defeated that the Nubian civilization never recovered – its great cities fell into ruins and its people reverted to living in huts. But the crusading idea never regained its initial power, not least because it was so

The Mongol century

Settled civilizations have always faced threats from nomadic peoples from agriculturally less promising areas. The Mongols in the 13th century were the most menacing.

The Mongols allied themselves in 1206 with other similar Turkish groups to form the most vital force in the world. Under Genghis Khan (which means 'prince of all that lies between the oceans') they ravaged Peking in 1215 before turning west and conquering Persia, Armenia, northern India and southern Russia. Genghis' son Ogedai Khan continued the campaign of conquest, as his armies devastated Poland and Russia (the only successful winter invasion of Russia in history) and defeated a Polish-German army in 1241.

The Mongols might have been a 'barbarian horde' but they were sophisticated in some respects. They were the first people in Europe to

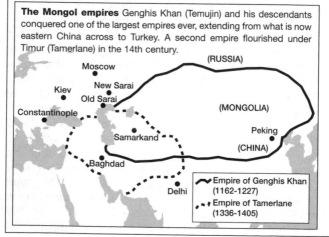

The Mongol empires Genghis Khan (Temujin) and his descendants conquered one of the largest empires ever, extending from what is now eastern China across to Turkey. A second empire flourished under Timur (Tamerlane) in the 14th century.

(RUSSIA)

Moscow

Kiev
New Sarai
Old Sarai
(MONGOLIA)

Constantinople

Samarkand
Peking

(CHINA)

Baghdad

Delhi

~ Empire of Genghis Khan (1162-1227)
- ■ - Empire of Tamerlane (1336-1405)

clearly manipulated by the Popes as a political tool.

The Christian Church in general was now losing its political grip. It was frequently at odds with the kings of Europe who resented the Church's wealth and independence. Childless people often left their lands to the Church which consequently accrued a great deal of property. And the monasteries paid taxes not to the king but to Rome, which meant that as much as a quarter of a country could be effectively independent of its temporal ruler. Not surprisingly,

use gunpowder in battle, an invention learned from the Chinese, and their military operations were planned with an intelligence far surpassing anything on the European side. They used spies to garner information and to decide when a country was ripe for attack. But in most other ways they were the ultimate in destructive terror. They would ruthlessly enslave any opponents who surrendered immediately. And everyone else was killed – regardless of age or sex. They were nomads who found urban life hard to understand – and responded by trying to wipe it out, as cities from Peking (now Beijing) to Kiev found to their cost.

The Mongol armies might well have conquered Western Europe had they tried. But they turned back because Ogedai's death caused a dispute over the succession. Subsequently they concentrated more on the East and by the middle of the century they had defeated the Sung empire and become rulers of China. In 1280 Kublai Khan formally assumed the title of emperor.

Meanwhile his brother Hulegu had been devastating Persia and Syria, capturing the Muslim capital of Baghdad; he too only turned back because of a dispute over succession. This conquest had a lasting result. Ever since the Sumerian civilization, Mesopotamia had maintained its agricultural fertility through an elaborate irrigation system. Hulegu Khan's Mongol forces destroyed not only cities and people but also the irrigation system which had supported them. As a result the region became prone to desertification and has remained agriculturally barren ever since.

But as with its forerunners the Mongol empire was short-lived: its eastern half became Buddhist and its western half converted to Islam. And the Mongols quickly outgrew their initial hostility to civilized life once they were in charge – both Kublai's China and Hulegu's Persia were as civilized and cultured as the regimes they had dispossessed. The Mongols were the last nomadic steppe people seriously to threaten the settled city-dwellers and cultivators. They were gradually brought under control in the centuries to follow by their powerful neighbors China and Russia. ■

Europe's monarchs were less than happy about this.

The Church also lost the sympathy of ordinary people. Priests and monks were steadily decreasing in quality – the Church was attracting recruits with more interest in earthly cash than heavenly reward. And they were literally a law unto themselves: they were immune to prosecution in civil courts and widely abused the privilege.

The Roman Church was further weakened by its own narrow-mindedness and vicious repression of dissent. Religious leaders like Waldo and St Francis of Assisi preached a return to the simple poverty of Jesus – their followers were brutally persecuted, imprisoned and murdered. The strict Dominicans were more to the taste of the Pope. They helped him set up an Inquisition to hunt heresy. Small wonder that throughout Europe the Church was feared and resented as often as it was the refuge of faith and hope.

1350 – Europe is finally reborn

The Church had to clamp down hard on dissent because its orthodoxies were being challenged by the 'Renaissance': a cultural and intellectual revival of Europe. People's horizons were widened as they came into contact with the cultures of the Chinese and the Muslims. As a result there was renewed interest in the great Greek texts, though at first people studied them slavishly instead of trying to develop the ideas. Universities sprang up in Bologna, Paris and Oxford and artistic work of fantastic beauty was produced in Italy, largely in celebration of the Christian God.

It was the arrival (at last) of printing and paper which made this exciting proliferation possible. Paper was used in China as early as the second century AD. The Arabs learned about it from the Chinese in the eighth century. But Europe did not produce paper of sufficient quality and quantity to publish books far and wide until the 15th century. Only then did reading become a more normal and widespread activity; and people began to write in their own language rather than in Latin.

1517 – Luther breaks down the door

Bibles were among the first books to be printed. This further undermined the authority of the Church because it meant priests no longer had a monopoly on the communication of religion. Papal influence waned still further when rival Popes appeared in Rome and Avignon, each damning and excommunicating the followers of the other. Apparently incapable of reforming itself, the Roman Church was ripe for religious revolution.

Martin Luther launched the most effective attack in Germany in 1517. He was a former monk who disputed Church orthodoxy via the printing press. Unfortunately he did not challenge the orthodox view of women. 'God formed her body to belong to a man,' said Luther, 'to have and to rear children... Let them bear children till they die of it. That is what they are for'.

Luther's religious ideas struck such a chord that within a generation most northern European countries had split with Rome and formed their own state churches based on this new Christianity called Protestantism. The monarchs of these countries were usually motivated more by resentment of Rome's power than religious conviction – and they swelled their coffers by confiscating Church property.

In the teeth of this onslaught the Catholic Church managed to regenerate itself and survive into the modern age. This was largely due to the work of a former Spanish soldier, St Ignatius of Loyola, who formed the Jesuits – a new missionary and educational body organized on almost military lines. But Rome was never as powerful again. ■

9 Glory and murder in the New World

Pyramid temples climb skyward. Mayan astronomers compute a sophisticated calendar. The Aztecs feed captives to their bloodthirsty gods. The Incas build a vast mountain empire. Then European ships appear on the horizon... and the story stops dead.

THE MONGOL EMPIRE helped pull Europe out of the Dark Ages – acting as a bridge with Chinese ideas. Europeans for the first time sensed that the world was a complete entity. It contained fascinatingly diverse peoples and things, but ultimately it was visitable, mappable, graspable. Travelers' tales like those of Marco Polo about the wonders of Kublai Khan's China stimulated the European imagination and sense of adventure. And by the 15th century, Europeans had discovered what the Chinese, Indians and Muslims

TOLTECS
TEOTIHUACAN
AZTECS
OLMECS
MAYA

MESO AMERICAN CIVILIZATIONS

already knew – that the world was round. This led a Genoese sailor called Columbus to consider reaching China by sailing west. At the end of his voyage in 1492 he landed in the Caribbean thinking he had reached India – and brought back as proof two native people along with gold and strange animals.

Europeans soon realized they had stumbled on a New World. But Columbus' mistake gave all native Americans the incongruous name of 'Indians' and labeled the Caribbean islands the West Indies.

Luckily the continent itself was given a less confusing name. Martin Waldseemuller produced an influential map of the world in 1507 and named the continent after his explorer friend Amerigo Vespucci. But the Europeans' New World was as much as 30,000 years old to the descendants of the first American pioneers.

6,000 BC – Magnificent mysteries

Settled, civilized life took longer to get into gear in the Americas. Agriculture had been practised in Central and South America for thousands of years before the Europeans arrived – from around 6,500 BC in the Andes and 500 years later in Mexico. But the practice of farming and of domesticating animals spread very slowly, probably because the population was not dense enough to require more food than could be got from gathering and hunting. People experimented with wild plants but cultivation was only a supplement to their normal diet. So it was at least 4,000 years after the discovery of agriculture that people settled in villages – three times as long as this transformation took in Africa and Asia. And the Old World's head start was to prove fatal for the people of the New.

The history of the ancient American civilizations is fascinating, with its priests and pyramids, and its complete independence from all the peoples introduced so far. But we still know little about it. In the absence of written records, everything rests on archaeology, and this cannot resolve certain mysteries – particularly why these cultures suddenly crumbled.

1,200 BC – Shattered godhead

The first known American civilization was that of the Olmecs, who expanded out of the tropical lowlands around the Gulf of Mexico about 1,200 BC. The Olmecs set the pattern to be followed elsewhere. A priestly élite governed a rigidly hierarchical state and they and their fine buildings were financed and labored on by ordinary people living in much more basic structures.

The Olmecs developed a hieroglyphic script and a

numerical system which spread all over the continent; and their pyramidal buildings were emulated everywhere. Their disappearance is a mystery, though they probably suffered defeat in war. In the fifth century BC their capital was destroyed and the enormous stone heads of their gods were smashed.

AD 600 – Time and the Maya

The next great people, the Maya, did not reach their heyday until about AD 600. They came from what is now Guatemala, Belize and Yucatan (Mexico) and built impressive pyramidal temples and multi-storied palaces which, like their Egyptian equivalents, must have cost Mayan laborers dear. Ordinary Mayans would have worked mainly as farmers: their hillside terracing was very sophisticated. So too were the Mayans' intellectual achievements. They further developed the Olmecs' numerical system, based on units of 20, and came up with the concept of zero not long after the Indians of the Old World. Much of their energy went into the recording of time and their 52-year astronomically based calendar was amazingly complex. This society also crumbled very suddenly – its cities were abandoned intact around 900, rather than destroyed, so they might have suffered an epidemic or perhaps an environmental catastrophe rather than an invasion.

650 – Megaliths and empires

There is yet more mystery attached to the first great Andean centers of Tiahuanaco and Huari, which were built around the seventh century. Around 800 these megalithic cities were deserted and the civilization disappeared without trace.

In Mexico an even larger city state had emerged between 100 and 750. Teotihuacan was, with more than 125,000 inhabitants, the biggest city in the New World (and larger than most in the Old). It covered 8 square miles/13 square kilometers and, if the remains are anything to go by, they had the most meticulous urban-planning department. Yet no written records have survived and it, too, was violently destroyed in the eighth century by an unknown force.

At this point Mexican history becomes marginally less shaky, thanks to the oral histories collected by a Spanish missionary in the 16th century. He discovered a repetition of the ancient pattern of the Old World, whereby fierce nomadic peoples attacked the more developed civilizations. The Toltecs were one of these, who established an empire in 10th-century Mexico.

1325 – Aztec blood
So too were the Aztecs who descended from the arid north in 1325 to found Tenochtitlan – modern Mexico City. The Aztecs served as mercenaries for a century before they felt able to carve out a niche for themselves. In 1428 they became rulers of their region and set about expanding through conquest; they would ally with one state to destroy another and then turn on their ally as well. Each conquered people had to pay a heavy tribute to finance the expansion of Tenochtitlan.

Tribute was often in the form of captives to be used for the amazing blood sacrifices which in their sheer scale and horror set the Aztecs apart. Tens of thousands of people would have their hearts ripped out – 20,000 women and men were killed in this way on just one occasion, the consecration of a new temple in 1487. In this sense the Aztec religion was deeply pessimistic – the gods had to be continually propitiated in blood if they were not to turn against their people.

This was a highly developed state which ruled as many as 25 million people – but it was an extremely cruel and ruthless one. There were frequent famines and peasant revolts in the 15th century and these increased after the priest Montezuma II was chosen as the new emperor in 1502. He increased the level of tribute which had to be paid, which caused resistance in neighboring states; and crop failures caused revolts against his authority at home. A sense of doom came over the land: a comet seen in 1510 was interpreted as an omen of the return of the old Toltec god Quetzalcoatl. He, according to mythology, had wanted the sacrifices to be symbolic ones of jade, butterflies and snakes. But he was expelled by priests who preferred human blood.

1519 – The conquistadors

The Spanish were able to capitalize on these disruptions when they landed from Cuba in 1519. Spain had already settled many of the islands of the Caribbean, and it was the mayor of Cuba's new capital Havana, Hernán Cortés, who led the expeditionary force of just 600 men which landed in Mexico. It started as it meant to go on, defeating local resistance with horses, guns, steel swords and armor. The Spanish seemed like gods with their immense firepower and different appearance. Local people, already resentful of Aztec rule, rallied to the Spanish army as they progressed towards Tenochtitlan. Montezuma was unsure as to whether or not this was the god Quetzalcoatl, so he received Cortés graciously, only to be rewarded by being taken captive. Full-scale war resulted when panicking soldiers massacred Aztecs at a religious service and the Spanish captured Tenochtitlan after a siege in 1521. The country was renamed New Spain and the tragic history of colonialism had begun.

1525 – Inca triumph and disaster

The Incas were the next to be conquered. They had risen to preeminence in the Andes from 1438 when their new king Pachacuti Inca had embarked on a series of extraordinarily successful conquests. Within 40 years this small highland group had built a huge empire embracing virtually the whole of the Andes region from modern Ecuador to Chile. The Incas were remarkably well-organized, not least in their engineering achievements – they built 9,000 miles of paved roads using sophisticated bridges and tunnels to link their capital Cuzco with the fringes of the empire. This was largely because, like all the other early South American peoples we know about, their society was rigidly hierarchical with a god king at the top and landless peasants at the bottom. Centralized state control was absolute and would have been envied by any fascist dictatorship of the 20th century.

But that control depended on the strong and undisputed rule of the god king, which is why the Incas were fatally weakened when civil war broke out over the succession in 1525. The 180 Spanish soldiers led by Francisco Pizarro arrived in the aftermath. Following the pattern in Mexico they kidnapped the new god-king Atahualpa during a parley, collected a ransom for his return and then murdered him. By the end of 1533 the Spanish had conquered Cuzco and gained control of the entire Inca empire – thanks partly to the foreign diseases they introduced which decimated the local population. From now on the Amerindian people would be marginalized, and absorbed by the incoming hordes of conquistadors.

SOUTH AMERICAN CIVILIZATIONS

1607 – The white death
The impact of the Spanish on the native peoples of Latin America is one of the most terrifying episodes in human history. It was far worse than the Black Death.

Glory and murder in the New World

There were perhaps 21 million Mexicans in 1519 but they had shrunk to 2.5 million by 1565 and just 1 million by 1607. The story in Peru was similar: only 1.5 million people remained where there had once been 11 million.

The comparison with the Black Death is apt. Most people were victims not of the sword but of disease. After thousands of years of separate development the Native Americans had no resistance to diseases of the Old World such as smallpox, measles or influenza.

But many also died laboring in the mines. They were whipped on to extract the silver that was the driving motive of Spanish colonization. They produced phenomenal wealth. By 1650, 16,000 tons of silver and 180 tons of gold objects had been shipped to Europe from the New World.

1650 – Slavery and worse
The Spanish Government, surprisingly enough, outlawed the enslavement of native people in 1542 – though it was soon forced by vested interests to relax its ruling. Indians continued to be viciously exploited for their labor in the mines and on agricultural plantations. But as they died off, African slaves were imported to replace them. These were provided by the Portuguese, who had been systematically slave trading since the 1440s – and with the special permission of the Pope since 1455 (an appalling episode in Christian history). By 1650 there were about 40,000 African slaves in Mexico and 30,000 in Peru. But this was small beer compared with the Caribbean, where British, French and Dutch plantations absorbed about 2,000,000 slaves in the 17th and 18th centuries.

Even more landed in Brazil. Portugal claimed Brazil in 1500 and within 50 years had started to cultivate sugar on large plantations. Work on a sugar plantation is among the hardest labor known to humans; it was, therefore, entirely the province of slaves. Between 1550 and 1800 Brazil alone probably absorbed 2.5

The Atlantic slave trade (1450-1870)

The Portuguese, British, French, Spanish and Dutch all transported slaves from Africa to the Americas and the Caribbean. It is estimated that a total of 12 million Africans were uprooted to work the European plantations. This chart shows the *annual* number of slaves transported, (in thousands) in the period 1450-1870. ■

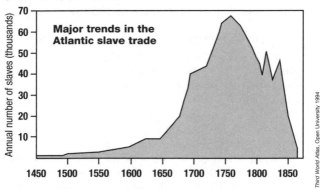

Major trends in the Atlantic slave trade

Third World Atlas, Open University 1994

million African slaves. Yet in 1800 its black population was still only one million.

Where did they go? Most died; a few escaped. Slave owners calculated that slaves working flat out started to produce pure profit after two years. But after five or six years they were worn out and new blood was needed. And it proved far more cost-effective to work people to death and replace them than to improve conditions and encourage them to have families. In all history there is no more appalling example of the power of moneymaking to corrupt human decency.

10 The hidden continent

In Africa the Bantu peoples harness hostile conditions. Great and golden civilizations arise in the West and South. And the Swahili traders meet with all comers from India and China. But the Europeans boost a deadly form of trade – in slaves.

EGYPT HAS LOOMED large in this story; while Kush, Nubia and Axum have at least poked their noses round the door. But the rest of Africa has not appeared at all: isolated by the enormous wastes of the Sahara from the currents of world history.

But there was one important and lucrative trade across the Sahara for well over a thousand years before European ships arrived. Camel trains carried gold northward – and it was the gold of West Africa which provided the fuel for the European Renaissance. The gold came from great civilizations, the history of which later Europeans did their best to ignore, so as not to disturb their notion that Africans were barbaric savages. Until some 3,000 years ago, Africa south of the Sahara was almost entirely populated by scattered groups who lived by trapping animals and gathering wild fruits or plants. But then Bantu-speaking people migrated out of the rainforests of West Africa. They had reached the Congo by about 500 BC, Kenya by about AD 100 and South Africa by about AD 300. Curiously enough this is one historical fact that we do need to know. During the apartheid era, many white South Africans claimed that the land was uninhabited by African Bantu-speaking farmers when the first Dutch settlers arrived in the 17th century. In fact the ancestors of peoples such as the Xhosa, Tswana and Zulu had been in South Africa for over a thousand years.

The African Bantu-speakers generally displaced or absorbed the hunter-gatherer people they encountered in order to clear small fields for cultivation and set up villages in the river valleys. They were coping with and taming the most difficult of environments. Although Africa is the birthplace of humanity, it is also the continent most hostile to human survival. And the African Bantu people's success in coping with conditions of disease, climate and topography that Europeans found daunting even into the 20th century is one of the major achievements of human development.

700 – The golden kings

But the first great African cities had emerged back in the heartland of West Africa. The most significant was the empire of Ghana. Muslim traders found it hugely impressive: a court which had grown rich by taxing the trans-Saharan trade. African empires differed from European ones like the Roman or the British. They were very tolerant of local customs; happy just to collect their taxes and be accorded ceremonial shows of loyalty. Ghana fell to nomadic invaders from Morocco in 1076 and never recovered its former magnificence.

The Mandinka were the next people to monopolize the lucrative Saharan trade. From the 13th century they carved out the empire of Mali which became one of the richest states in the world west of India and China.

It reached the full height of its power under Kankan Musa in the 14th century. When Kankan Musa made a

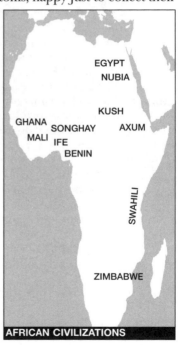

EGYPT
NUBIA

KUSH

GHANA   SONGHAY   AXUM
MALI   IFE
        BENIN

SWAHILI

ZIMBABWE

AFRICAN CIVILIZATIONS

pilgrimage to Mecca in 1324 he stopped off in Cairo en route and he and his entourage splashed so much gold around that its price on the Cairo market had still not recovered 12 years later.

Kankan Musa's predecessor is reputed to have set off into the Atlantic with 2,000 ships in search of the land on the other side. The expedition never returned – not surprisingly, since the prevailing wind would have helped them west but not allowed them to sail back in the ships they had at the time. Did these black Africans reach the Americas two centuries before Columbus?

1300 – Beauty in the rainforest

Mali lost overall control of the trade routes from around 1450. Power was assumed by the Songhay, who held it until a sudden invasion from Morocco in the 1590s. But by then these empires of the grasslands were being rivaled for magnificence by civilizations based in the West African rainforests nearer the coast. Two of the most significant were the Yoruba city of Ife and the Edo city of Benin.

By around 1300 the Yoruba had developed enough of a food surplus for an élite to emerge. And local artists began to produce for them works of art of great beauty. These bronze and terracotta heads of kings are the only surviving relics of Ife's former glory. As always it is only the concentration of wealth and the exploitation of labor that allows future generations to be impressed by past greatness. This is as true of sub-Saharan Africa as it is of the Pyramids of Egypt, the palaces of Europe and the temples of Asia.

The Edo capital of Benin arose as a great trading city probably as early as the 11th century and had reached its peak by about 1450. A Dutch merchant who visited Benin just before 1600 was greatly impressed by its size – larger than Amsterdam, he thought. Another Dutch observer praised its 'good laws' and 'well-organized police'.

The myth of African ignorance

Africa the savage, the untamable. Africa the heart of darkness. Africa swarming with pygmies and cannibals.

Western attitudes reflected this comic-book view of the continent until surprisingly recently. Europeans strenuously denied all of Africa's independent achievements and its great civilizations; they needed to believe Africans were children, requiring the firm rule and superior intellect of white people to progress.

The root of this view, as with modern racism, lay in slavery. Europeans rationalized slavery by considering Africans less than human; and generations of Europeans only came into contact with black people as degraded drudges on brutal plantations. The greatest European philosophers were infected with the notion of black African inferiority: Hume was 'apt to suspect the Negroes to be naturally inferior to the Whites'; while Hegel states that the African 'exhibits the natural man in his completely wild and untamed state. There is nothing harmonious with humanity in this type of character'.

Darwin's theory of evolution also spawned a pseudo-science which bolstered this consensus. This put Africans on the bottom rung of a natural hierarchy that stretched upward through Asians to the glorious apogee of the white European. And it was further reinforced by the same kind of self-serving motive that had surrounded the slave trade: if Europeans were to invade and partition Africa it would help them construe this not as the immoral greed that it certainly was but rather as a moral duty aimed at civilizing barbaric inferiors.

Any historical evidence of great African civilizations had to be dismissed – for it was both confusing and threatening. The 14th-century Shona palace of Great Zimbabwe provides the classic example. When white explorers first came across this they simply could not believe it had been built by Africans. One theory said it was the land of King Solomon's Mines, another said the Queen of Sheba had lived here, still another that it was a Phoenician settlement. Similarly in 1910 when seven magnificent terracotta sculptures were discovered in Nigeria there were two theories about them: one, that they were products of a long-lost Greek colony; and two, that they were echoes of even longer-lost Atlantis.

So until the middle of the 20th century the Africans' history had been left completely blank, as if they had formed no part of the human family. And for that reason the uncovering of the African heritage is one of the great cultural adventures of our time. ∎

1300 – Lord of ravaged lands

When Portuguese sailors investigated the east coast of Africa, they learned of two other significant civilizations: the Swahili and Great Zimbabwe. The Arabs were the first fully to exploit the sea-trading potential of the east coast. After about 700, the local African trading culture became entirely Muslim and was called Swahili, from the Arabic word for 'shore' which in a slightly different form still describes the southern shores of the Sahara – the Sahel.

These Swahili people acted as intermediaries between Africans from the interior and ships from India and China. The Africans exchanged gold and ivory for imported cotton garments and luxury goods – evidence that a thriving and peaceful trade had been carried on between distant lands for centuries before the Europeans hijacked the business. The Swahili took a cut from the trade for themselves and with it built cities in architectural styles that expressed their union of the African with the Arab.

But who were these people bringing goods from the interior? The Portuguese heard of 'the great kingdom of the Monomotapa'. This had arisen around 1100 when ancestors of the Shona people in modern Zimbabwe began building in stone and developing small kingdoms. As they began to trade gold for Asian luxuries the wealth of these kings grew and they built large palaces. The largest of these was that known now as Great Zimbabwe (the word itself means 'royal court'), built around 1300. The massive stone walls still stand today. This was abandoned around 1425 by the Shona king Mutota, who moved to a new capital and then set about conquering the peoples around him, with sufficient success to gain the title Mwana-Mutapha (lord of ravaged lands), the words Portuguese heard as Monomotapa.

1415 – Enter the Portuguese

So there had been civilizations in both West and East Africa before the Europeans came. The Portuguese adventurer Vasco da Gama was one of the first to arrive. His initial ground-breaking voyage around the Cape went straight on to India and inflicted no harm on East Africa. But his second was aimed at conquest:

the great Swahili cities of Kilwa and Mombasa were looted and destroyed. The king of Mombasa lamented that after the Portuguese had left he had found 'no living thing (in the city), neither man nor woman, young nor old, nor child however small. All who had failed to escape had been killed and burned'.

West Africans were less vulnerable to the Portuguese as their cities were far from the coast. And at first their trade with them was a business relationship between equals: the Europeans built trading stations on the coast but paid rent for the land and the African kingdoms were pleased to find a new trading frontier. The king of Benin took Portuguese soldiers into his service and in 1486 sent an ambassador to Lisbon. And the son of the King of Kongo (in modern Angola) was invited to Portugal, trained for the priesthood and made a bishop by the Pope before returning home in 1518.

We are used to thinking of Africa as a developmental straggler. But the technological gap between West Africa and Europe was pretty small in the 15th century. The Europeans had better guns and ships than the Africans and they were certainly more ruthless in warfare. But the Africans were distinctly superior in political terms to the Europeans (with the exception of the Dutch). Indeed none of the visiting Europeans would have felt they were visiting natural inferiors: that pernicious idea came much later.

1460 – Descent into slavery

For 30 years the Portuguese sailed home with ships full of gold and the African rulers were just as happy with the cottons, woolens and brass that they received in exchange. And from the beginning the Portuguese were allowed to take small numbers of slaves, since slavery was part of the African disciplinary code – the normal punishment for crime was enslavement, so African states had a supply of such 'disposable' people that they were quite happy to pass on to the Portuguese.

By the 1460s about 700 black slaves were being carried back each year to Europe where they became very fashionable as domestic servants.

This might give the impression that slavery was an African tradition foreign to Europeans. In fact slavery had been a part of the European business scene for centuries before the Portuguese touched the Gold Coast. Christian raiders kidnapped non-Christians from Eastern Europe and sold them as slaves to the Franks; the Franks often sold them on to Muslim princes in North Africa. Much of the prosperity of the great merchant cities of Venice and Genoa – and hence some of the money that fueled the Renaissance – was built on the slave trade. Indeed the very word 'slave' derives from the Slavic people who were the main European victims of the trade at this time. On Mediterranean islands such as Cyprus, the old Roman tradition of plantation agriculture had been revived, with slave labor providing sugar for the European market.

1525 – A trickle becomes a flood

The slave trade began to get out of control in Africa in the latter half of the 15th century when the Portuguese set up sugar plantations with slave labor on Atlantic islands such as São Tomé. The African rulers could not supply anywhere near enough criminals for this so mass kidnapping raids began. The King of Kongo, accustomed to more polite relations, begged his counterpart in Portugal in 1525 to stop the raids 'because it is our will that in these kingdoms there should not be any trade in slaves or outlet for them'. He was ignored.

São Tomé remained a slave island well into the 20th century. But the real tragedy began when the New World started to demand slaves. In 1510 the first blacks were sold in the West Indies and by 1515 slave-grown Caribbean sugar was being sold in Spain. By the middle of the 17th century there were more than 40 slave fortresses on the coast of West Africa, run by the

British, French and Dutch as well as the Portuguese. Not all these slaves were seized at the point of a gun. African rulers had to choose between providing enough slaves or forgoing all European imports and too often they chose the first because much of their power had come to rest upon the second. If they could not buy enough captives from their neighbors they would simply seize them by military force.

1800s – The terrible equation

This was the largest forced migration in history and it laid the foundations of our chronically unequal modern world. African slavery fed the European economic growth that spiraled into the Industrial Revolution – as well as providing the United States with a kick-start it could never have hoped for by the sweat of its settlers' brows alone.

And on the African side of this terrible equation there was simply desolation. The experience of being ripped from your home, of being squeezed onto a deck with no room to move, of lying in chains for weeks amid your own excrement, of staggering out at the other end into a half-life of backbreaking labor at the crack of a whip – all of this is beyond imagination.

Yet it is written in the bones of the black people descended from the slaves. And it is written too in the bones of the African continent itself. Over the four centuries of the slave trade, between 10 and 12 million Africans were sold in the Americas and about 2 million died along the way. All of those taken were young and healthy. This removed not only those most able to have children but also those most able to work. The ground for development was undermined and Africa is still counting the cost today.

11 Shadow of the Sun King

Europe's warlord leaders become obsessed with their divinity and see their own beautiful reflection in the wealth and glory of their nations. Ordinary people are called upon to dig deeper so that rulers and their palaces might look even more splendid. They begin to get restive.

EUROPE'S OBSESSION WITH the idea of a Holy Roman Empire had dictated policy, national ambition and warmongering for centuries. It had a last great flowering in the person of the Emperor Charles V but died with him in 1558. The Austrian branch of his descendants, the Habsburgs, continued to call themselves emperors and empresses. But in practice they were no more than monarchs. And this was the new European obsession: absolute monarchy. There were a few exceptions to this rule – Holland had become a republic that actively encouraged free speech; Switzerland was a collection of republican cantonments independent of the ebbs and flows of European politics (as it has remained into the 21st century).

1643 – Personal power gone mad
But elsewhere the decline of the Pope's power permitted national queens and kings to assert personal authority, to equate the good of the nation with their own interests. The epitome of the absolute monarch was France's Louis XIV. His father and grandfather had already concentrated power in their own hands more effectively than any other sovereigns in Europe. But in Louis' reign (1643-1715) not only did all power become centralized into the hands of one man (*'L'état c'est moi,'* he said in a famous phrase – 'the state is me') but also every recognized glory and virtue was thought to reside in him.

He was known as the Sun King, and all other people

were his satellites. Only he could bring light. If he encouraged culture it was only in order that it might redound to his own greater magnificence. If he schemed diplomatically and sent his subjects to war it was only that his own brilliance might be multiplied by conquest. If he raised taxes from ordinary people it was not to improve their lot but to finance ever more extravagant luxury at his Versailles court. And absolute power meant just that: the lowliest of his subjects found they could barely relieve themselves without finding that Louis had decreed they should do it in a particular way.

1645 – The divine right of kings

Most rulers of Europe from the 16th to the 18th centuries were similarly obsessed with personal power. In a way this was a refinement of the ancient idea of a god-king. They were not claiming absolute power on the basis of personal ability (though some doubtless thought this would have been reason enough). They saw themselves as embodying the divine will of the Christian God upon their patch of earth. Charles I was perhaps the most passionate of believers in this 'divine right of kings'. He ruled what, after the union of Scotland and its neighbors under his father, James, was now effectively Britain.

But the trend towards absolute monarchy was by no means the only political development of the age. A group of Protestant landowners who dominated the British Parliament were so appalled by the King's fecklessness and Catholic tendencies that they staged a revolutionary civil war which ended in 1649 in Charles' execution and the declaration of a republic.

This was one of the first great political fruits of the wider availability of paper, of Protestantism's belief in individual conscience and of the spread of education beyond the priesthood. The more people learned, the more the old molds began to crack. And the notion of scores of different petty rulers each claiming to be

God's representative on earth was so ludicrous that it was only a matter of time before the battle for political power was joined. At this point the earliest 'socialists' started to emerge: movements like the Diggers and Levellers in Britain and, rather later, thinkers like Saint Simon in France. From Plato onwards there had been individuals who could imagine better ways of organizing the world. But these new Europeans were the first people to see an egalitarian society as a practical possibility in their own time.

Even these idealists, though, were worlds apart from the common people of Europe – they were wealthy landowners who may not have included the lowest social classes in their notion of equality (just as few 19th-century campaigners for the 'universal franchise' believed women should be included).

1660 – Tax-free aristocrats

All the great buildings of the age, all the fine costumes and artistic wonders, were paid for, as throughout history, from the labor of ordinary people.

But there was now a crucial difference: people could see this was making them worse off. The more opulent and magnificent the courts and country houses of their 'betters' became, the greater the sacrifices everyone else had to make. In France, Prussia and Spain, the aristocracy did not even have to pay taxes, while particularly in Eastern Europe the plight of the peasantry was worsening rather than improving (in Prussia, for instance, all children of the tied peasants known as 'serfs' had to work as unpaid servants for their lord for four years).

The tax burden fell more and more, though, on the emerging middle classes of the towns. And they were the most likely to wrest government from hereditary monarchies. Not quite yet, though. For even the British experiment with republicanism had been only temporary – Charles I's son, Charles II, returned to the throne in 1660 and the British ruling class proved

The Ottoman Empire

The West has never understood Islam. This was true during the Crusades and it is sadly little less true now.

Nor have some Western historians taken much interest in Muslim empires, even when they last for five centuries, as did that of the Ottoman Turks. This originated in a small state ruled by a chief called Uthman at the start of the 14th century. Over the next 50 years this country steadily expanded at the expense of its neighbors, causing such alarm among Christian Europeans that another crusading army was raised and annihilated at Nicopolis in 1396.

During the 15th century the Ottomans became a significant world power. Their most spectacular early conquest was of Constantinople, the Christian bastion which had survived all threats since its establishment as the eastern capital of the Roman empire by the Emperor Constantine. Faced with a bombardment from the first siege cannon, Constantinople fell in 1453. It was turned into the Islamic center it has remained to this day and became by far the largest city in Europe (about 500,000) under its new name of Istanbul.

The news of Constantinople's fall sent shock waves through Christendom, yet no-one seemed able to resist the Ottoman expansion. In the mid-16th century, under Suleiman the Magnificent, the Ottoman Empire reached its furthest extent, ruling the whole of North Africa, all the Muslim holy cities, and much of Eastern Europe – around a million square miles/2.6 million square kilometers. If the Ottoman expansion had continued deeper into Europe, our modern world might have looked very different. In the end the crunch came in 1683 at Vienna, when an Ottoman army of 200,000 held the Austrian capital under siege for three months before being beaten back by a combined European force.

After that the Ottoman Empire remained static, becoming more interesting to Western historians when it started to decline and could be labeled the 'Sick Man of Europe'. Yet there had been a succession of high-caliber Ottoman sultans; and their architectural achievements were spectacular. The Empire decayed only when it ceased to expand. Indeed its eventual collapse early in the 20th century was because it had become too secure – feeling no need to look outwards, it failed to respond to the aggressive European developments in science and technology. ∎

so fond of monarchy that when they next deposed a king in 1688 they invited a Dutch duke – William of Orange – to replace him.

1700 – The Enlightened Despots

The heyday of European monarchy lasted through the 17th and 18th centuries as even the newest nations aped Louis XIV's model. Russia had shaken off centuries of Mongol domination in 1480 to become a recognizable country for the first time under the Grand Duke of Moscow. His grandson Ivan the Terrible took the imperial title of Czar in 1547 in honor of his claim to the Byzantine half of the old Holy Roman Empire. But Russia was still separate from the rest of Europe and retained its distance until the reign of Peter the Great (1689-1725). He was eager to import the latest artistic and philosophical ideas from France and Germany as well as shipbuilding techniques from Holland and Britain. This naturally involved building his own spectacular equivalent to Versailles, as did Frederick the Great, king of the newly emerging German nation of Prussia.

Along with Maria-Theresa and Joseph II of Austria-Hungary and Catherine the Great of Russia, these were the 'Enlightened Despots', who leavened their ruthless autocracy and pointless warmongering with a lively interest in art, music and philosophy. They were the best of a bad lot of rulers who can claim some small credit for the flowering of intellectual and artistic talent that included Bach and Mozart. But who knows what other potential geniuses were hidden among the masses of ordinary people across Europe whose living conditions were of little pressing concern to their rulers?

12 The American way

Native North Americans – First Peoples – dispute their land with European invaders, who then battle for their own independence. Latin America too secures its political liberty. Only Canada remains a colony. Freedom becomes the most important American word – but the native people are not allowed to translate it.

THE INDIGENOUS GROUPS in the northern half of the Americas had come to terms with hostile environments. The Inuit people caught (and still catch) seals in the frozen tundra of the far north, whereas people in the arid deserts of the south had to survive by gathering seeds. In between the two, the groups in the wide open spaces hunted mammoths, camels and horses so effectively that these became extinct. And perhaps this served as an ecological lesson to the first Americans. For they had, by the time Europeans arrived, developed an environmentally sustainable lifestyle which we in the post-industrial world are only now learning to admire.

Only the peoples in the fertile eastern forests settled down to farm. As maize cultivation grew, they built collections of elaborate homes for the tribal élite and these turned into towns. Cahokia, near the present St Louis, was the largest of these. This was North America's first city with a population of around 40,000 by the year 1000.

1607 – Gold-diggers and slave wives

The earliest Europeans to disturb this calm were men on the look-out for gold and silver. The British set up Jamestown, Virginia, in 1607 and the French Quebec in the following year. Women initially arrived only under duress – paupers and orphan girls were shipped across the Atlantic and sold to the rough male pioneers. But eventually the ships started depositing whole communities of both women and men, as when Puritans fled religious persecution in 17th-century England. To the great misfortune of the peoples whose home it already was, these Puritans' belief in Christian values did not extend to peaceful coexistence with the native people.

The two groups had very different attitudes to land. The indigenous Americans saw the land as not just a home but a nurturing element of the universe – they could no more think of owning land than of owning the air. To the settlers this new territory was like any other – there to be claimed, fenced in and controlled.

The European settlers, with their superior firepower, ruthlessly pushed the Native Americans on the eastern seaboard deeper into the interior – usually gaining a hold by allying with and aiming one group against another, as in Quebec where the French helped the Iroquois to destroy the Hurons.

1776 – American Revolution

By 1760, settlement had still not extended beyond a thin coastal strip running from Maine to Georgia, 140 years after the Pilgrim Parents (the 18 women are rarely mentioned) had founded New Plymouth and the first African slaves had been set ashore. Britain claimed most of this (despite many communities of French, Swedes and Dutch) and a war in Europe also gave it the chance to seize France's American and Canadian colonies.

The British ruling class regarded this as a final victory. But they failed to recognize a more independent spirit in the colonies and tried to raise new taxes from the settlers while forbidding them to move further west. London, it seemed, planned to sell the rest of America to the highest bidder – a sale of national assets which no privatizing politician of the present could match. The settlers were outraged and violent popular demonstrations broke out. Britain cracked down and eventually killed American

Outgrowing slavery

Slavery was abolished by most Western countries during the 19th century – after centuries of reaping the profits from it. The credit for this traditionally goes to individuals of conscience such as William Wilberforce in Britain. And there were certainly many liberal campaigners against slavery whose passionate opposition helped bring it to an end.

But governments outlawed the practice chiefly for pragmatic reasons. Slaves might not have been well cared for but they had to be given accommodation and food as well as kept under guard. The coming of factories with the Industrial Revolution made this trouble unnecessary: it was easier to exploit people's labor in return for cash payments and leave them 'free' to find the necessities of life themselves. This was also why Britain led the way – because it was the first nation in the world to industrialize.

The most dramatic end to slavery came in the US. The Southern states had been founded on African slavery – growing cotton for the mills of New England and Europe. The Northern states, however, had embraced the Industrial Revolution and were continually revitalized by immigration from Europe. They thus had no need of African slaves and from 1833 the anti-slavery movement began to gather support in the North. As a result the Southern states began to talk of seceding from the Union to protect a slave-based industry which was making them huge profits – and even to dream about developing a slave-based empire in the Caribbean and Central America.

The 1860 election dramatized the debate. It was won by Abraham Lincoln, the candidate opposed to the extension of slavery. Before he had even been inaugurated, some Southern states had withdrawn from the Union and effectively declared war. The US Civil War is often seen as a crusade against slavery and there were certainly people in Union ranks who were fighting because of their passionate opposition to it – including many black people. But much more important to Lincoln and the North was the preservation of the United States.

The war dragged on for four years and one million people were killed before, in 1865, the South was forced to surrender and slavery was abolished. But racism itself could not be abolished so easily and it ensured that black people in the South remained scandalously deprived and maltreated for the next hundred years. ∎

protesters. Even then the Americans were anxious to compromise but were rebuffed at every stage by the British Government and a full-scale war resulted. This soon became a war of independence. The rebel states issued their Declaration of Independence in 1776 and finally broke loose seven years later after inflicting two major defeats on British armies.

At first it looked as though the newly independent states would form European-sized countries. The character and interests of Puritan New England were after all very different from those of the slave-owning plantation farmers in the South. But fragmentation would have been dangerous, given the continued hostility of Britain and France. Instead a remarkably advanced federal republican constitution was drawn up in 1788 and a sense of nationhood was promoted by another war with Britain in 1812 – though the differences between North and South festered in the background, waiting to be resolved.

1808 – Rebellion in Latin America

The same enlightened ideas (many imported from Europe) of liberty and democracy that had inspired the North Americans to seek independence had been received with equal enthusiasm in the Spanish colonies of Latin America. And these countries were also encouraged by the success of the rebels farther north. In the 20 years from 1808 most were to achieve independence.

Spain was distracted during this time by a war with the French in Europe. This encouraged a band of British military adventurers to seize Buenos Aires in 1808. But they were then ousted themselves by a popular rebellion which proved capable of defending itself. Ordinary people fought with anything that came to hand from muskets to stink bombs. Argentina's independence was unchallenged by either Spain or Britain from then on – an achievement which reverberated around the whole continent.

But independence required a more bitter fight elsewhere in Spanish America. In Mexico there was an Indian peasant rebellion for land rights in 1808 which was put down by a nervous colonial élite with the help of middle-class liberals whose sympathy for independence did not extend to genuine revolution.

They gained an independence more to their taste in 1821 when even the most powerful and wealthy Mexicans wanted to break with Spain because it had become infected with dangerously liberal ideas which might have threatened their privileged position.

1816 – The Liberator...

In most of South America the independence movements were led by educated *criollos* – people of direct European descent. The key figure here was a Venezuelan, Simón Bolívar. In 1816 he launched a long military campaign which was to bring most of the continent its independence.

From Venezuela one revolutionary army fought its way down towards Peru. Meanwhile a second army had been working up from the south, aiming to protect Argentina's independence by expelling the Spanish from neighboring states. This second force captured Lima, Spain's South American capital, in 1821. By 1825 nothing of Spain's vast empire was still in its hands except the Caribbean islands of Cuba and Puerto Rico.

1825... and the Dictators

But there was to be no United States of South America. The regional differences were too great and they shaped the countries that appear on the map today. What is more, the character of the liberation movements helped determine the social structure of modem Latin America. In that sense the failed Indian rebellion in Mexico was symptomatic. Power and wealth remained in the hands of the privileged *criollos* with the *mestizos* (people of Spanish and Indian descent) beneath them and the native population scraping its subsistence from the land as it had done since the arrival of the Spanish.

But more than this: even Bolívar, originally imbued with liberal idealism, came to believe that Latin American conditions required dictatorial government;

the people were not ready for democracy. So when the new republican constitutions were drawn up they all allowed for presidential dictatorships in times of crisis or social disorder. Latin American politics has been dogged ever since by strong rulers (or *caudillos*) imposing order at all costs.

1822 – An American emperor

Brazil, meanwhile, remained under Portuguese control. Indeed after Napoleon's invasion of Portugal in 1807 the royal family actually ruled from Brazil. When the royal court returned to Portugal in 1821 Prince Pedro, the heir to the throne, stayed behind and was persuaded to declare an independent empire in 1822 – Brazilians were not prepared to return to being a mere colony. But the idea of hereditary monarchy did not take root in America and Brazil's imperial experiment ended when it became a republic in 1889.

1830 – Justifying genocide

Once the US was independent, settlement expanded fast, helped by the new steamboats from around 1810 and railways from 1830. The new technology arrived from Britain just when it was needed. Without it the US would never have embraced the whole breadth of the continent.

But the land still had to be seized from its original inhabitants. And the high ideals of the US Constitution – life, liberty and the pursuit of happiness – did not apply to the native peoples. Instead a propaganda campaign was started – one which was to infect almost every Hollywood Western made before the 1960s. The 'Indians' were described as primitive and barbaric (like the Africans at the time of slavery); they committed violent atrocities for no reason (like the Turks at the time of the Crusades); they cut off white people's scalps as war prizes (in fact it was the British King George III who had offered a cash reward for each Indian scalp brought in as proof of a 'kill'). The propaganda stirred up settlers' anger and provided a specious justification for genocide.

1835 – Cavalry and Indians

Some Native American groups fought back. They had gained horses from the Spanish and guns from the French and English, and the Apache and Lakota (or Sioux) in particular used them to great advantage. But the firepower of the settlers was inevitably superior and Indians were forcibly removed from their ancestral homes. In the 1830s, for example, 50,000 Cherokees from Georgia were gathered into prison camps and sent on a winter march to reservations set aside for them in Oklahoma. Many of them did not survive the ordeal.

The reservations were specially sited in lands which white people did not want – and if native people broke out of the reservations they were decimated by army machine guns. Some resisted more than others: the Lakota declared war in defense of their home in the Black Hills, in which settlers had discovered gold. They wiped out a detachment of US cavalry under Custer but suffered from a vicious backlash and were finally defeated at the Battle of Wounded Knee in 1890. By this time less than 500,000 remained of the 4,500,000 native people who had inhabited North America in 1500.

13 The power and plenty of Asia

Europeans pirate their way into the Indian Ocean and encounter India and China. They are suitably amazed. India is 'the land of wealth abounding' says a Portuguese poet; while according to an Italian writer 'there is no kingdom greater, or more populous, or more abundant in all good things' than China.

THE CHINESE EMPEROR Yung-lo sent a fleet of 63 ships and 28,000 sailors as far as the Swahili east coast of Africa in 1413. But this was no act of war, merely a promotional stunt aimed at selling Yung-lo as the greatest ruler in the world. Vasco da Gama, in contrast, had only four ships and 500 sailors when he entered the Indian Ocean at the end of the same century – yet he made war with a vengeance and stole whatever riches he could in the name of the Portuguese king.

This says a lot about the different attitudes of Asia and Europe. When the Portuguese – and in their wake the Dutch, Spanish and British – found their way into the Indian Ocean they set up fortified trading stations and tried to control sea trade by a mixture of piracy and protection racketeering.

But when they dealt with the great civilizations of India and China they had to be more humble – and pay for what they took. Most of the gold and silver from the Americas found its way eventually to India and China, since the Europeans had little else to offer in return for the spices, silks and other oriental luxuries they wanted.

Asia was streets ahead of Europe in both wealth and production. The ceramic factories of Nanking in China produced a million pieces of fine pottery a year, mostly for export – and with different patterns to fit the tastes of their European and Islamic buyers. The cotton weavers of Gujarat in India produced three million pieces a year for export. Indeed the most powerful monarchs in the world at the end of the 17th century were not Louis XIV or Peter the Great but the Chinese emperor, K'ang-hsi (1662-1722), and the Indian Mughal emperor, Aurangzeb (1658-1707). China and India had about 150 million inhabitants in 1750, each of them twice the population of Europe.

1368-1644 – Ming monk and bandit

China followed a familiar pattern after the death of Kublai Khan. A series of natural calamities (including the same bubonic plague that had devastated Europe) was followed by peasant revolts. The latest dynasty to emerge from this was the Ming. It was led by the first and only peasant in Chinese history to become emperor: Chu Yuan-chang was born into grinding poverty and worked as a Buddhist monk and a bandit before becoming a rebel military commander.

China's population doubled and the economy boomed in the two centuries of Ming rule. And what is still the most famous and expensive porcelain in the world started to be produced for export. But the Ming emperors, despite their peasant origins, were indifferent to the plight of the poor and shut themselves away inside Peking's Forbidden City. They paid the usual price in 1580 when another peasant revolt followed a series of droughts, famines and epidemics.

This time the rebellion coincided with an invasion by Manchurian peoples. The imperial forces were caught in a pincer movement. The last Ming emperor hanged himself as the rebel army reached Peking in 1644. But the rebel victory was short-lived. The invaders seized the capital from them and repressed all resistance, setting up the even more iron-handed Ch'ing dynasty which was to last until 1911 – right down to The Last Emperor.

1644-1800s – The greatest rebels

Not that the Ch'ing were left in peace. The sheer assertiveness of Chinese peasants over the centuries has been astonishing. In the history of other countries you can usually refer unambiguously to 'The Peasants' Revolt', whereas in China barely a generation passed without a major uprising. The modern Chinese Communists may have been no less authoritarian than the emperors, but they have suffered no such popular rebellions because they distributed food and wealth relatively equally. If the gap between rich and poor continues to widen as a result of the current obsession with the free market (and it is estimated that China's accession to the terms of the World Trade Organization will cost 40 million jobs), then the age-old patterns might yet return.

The imperial administrators, the 'mandarins', of the Ch'ing period became increasingly resistant to change – and bequeathed their name (and attitudes) to the 'Yes, Minister' civil servants of the modern West. They were uninterested in trade, except as a source of silver, and treated diplomatic missions with the utmost contempt. The British and Russians had become addicted to Chinese tea but they could find nothing that the Chinese wanted until the British introduced an addiction of their own – opium.

1526-1806 – Mughal India

The Mughal empire in India was established in 1526 by Mongol descendants of Genghis Khan. It was the most cultured of Muslim dynasties and built some of the most magnificent mosques and palaces in the world, including the Taj Mahal.

The Mughals depended on the tax from 150 million farmers. And for a century and a half they managed not to overburden their subjects while promoting their own wealth and culture – their miniature paintings are amongst the finest artistic achievements of Islam. But the emperor Aurangzeb upset the balance with expensive military campaigns and a series of rebellions by Sikhs and Hindus weakened the empire further.

The Persians took advantage of this and attacked Delhi in 1739 – leaving 30,000 dead. And they took the Mughals' fabled Peacock Throne back to Persia when they left.

The British East India Company stepped into the void. They exploited local divisions to gain control of the trading towns of Calcutta and Madras and managed to hijack the income from all land taxes in Bengal. This lucrative arrangement allowed the Company to support a highly trained army capable of challenging any power in India. By 1806 the whole of India was under either direct or indirect control of a private British company. Eat your heart out, General Motors.

14 *Liberté, Égalité, Fraternité* – Liberty, Equality, Brotherhood

France is convulsed by revolution – and the idealistic disease shows signs of spreading. But the Revolution is hijacked by a megalomaniac soldier, so the Old Order can breathe a sigh of relief. The pack remains unshuffled and kings and queens are dealt out all around the table.

THE OLD EUROPE was beginning to crack. People who were unable to survive on the land were flooding into the towns and cities. This was partly because population was rising fast but also because fields and estates were increasingly fenced in by rich landowners to finance their profligate lifestyles.

In some ways this parallels events in the Third World today which has rapid population growth and migration as well as a concentration of wealth in the hands of a few. Nowadays there is the added factor that the money extracted from the land is also being exported to the West. But in the 18th century a peasant did not have to look very far to see where a country's wealth was piling up.

1789 – The French Revolution

France was the epitome of the Old Europe of kings and queens, dukes and princesses. The aristocracy was completely exempt from tax, while the middle class and the poor were required to sustain the country in peace and war – not to mention keeping the Royal Family in its accustomed style.

In 1789 King Louis XVI met with representatives of lords, clergy and commons to discuss his overspending problems. The commoners – the only ordinary taxpayers present – were understandably anxious to see a change in approach and decided to form a National Assembly to keep the King in check.

Louis was outraged by this suggestion and called up troops from the provinces. But this time a judicious execution or two was not going to do the trick: the proposers of the National Assembly had the ordinary people of Paris behind them and they stormed the Bastille fortress, a hated symbol of royal power. They were led by a woman dressed as an Amazon, Théroigne de Méricourt, who later headed 8,000 women on a march to Versailles in protest at a bread shortage. The revolution spread into the provinces. Many aristocrats were murdered or driven into exile.

The National Assembly set about the urgent task of creating a new social order from amidst all the habits and injustices of the old. Plato had thought such a thing possible 2,300 years previously but this was probably the first time that it had been tried in practice (the US had declared their republic earlier but had the advantage of writing on a blank sheet).

The revolutionaries had a good try. Serfdom, aristocratic titles and tax exemptions were all abolished; torture, arbitrary imprisonment and persecutions for heresy were outlawed; new law courts and regional administrations were established. But not much was done for women, despite the major part they had played in the Revolution. *A Declaration of the Rights of Woman* was published in protest by Olympe de Gouges in 1791.

But even the Rights of Man were under threat that year: the armies of Austria and Prussia gathered on the eastern frontier following a plot between the Royal Family and aristocratic exiles. The whole of France flared up in passionate indignation; the remarkable de Méricourt attacked the royal palace with another battalion of Amazons; war was declared against all comers; France became a republic and the King was executed for treason against his people.

1791 – Idealism and terror
Any ideas of democratic gradualism were set aside in

the crisis. The high principles of the new France had to be defended for the sake of all humanity. Both women and men went to war enthusiastically for an ideal that transcended national interest – probably for the first time since the Crusades. They were prepared to accept all kinds of hardship and the French armies carried the day everywhere: by the end of 1791 they were at war with virtually all of Europe, determined to export their republicanism to every quarter.

But in France itself the same revolutionary enthusiasm took a negative turn. A climate of suspicion arose in which the executions included not just former aristocrats but also many innocent people. Much was done in the sincere belief that the Revolution had to be strictly protected, that the new world had to be cleansed by the fire that destroyed the old. But the idealistic popular impulse went astray and great revolutionaries went unnecessarily to the guillotine, the feminist de Gouges among them. This climate of terror was succeeded in 1794 by a calmer approach at home.

The foreign wars continued. But over the years they lost their special missionary quality and became simply expansionist wars of a kind which the old kings would have understood.

1799 – Napoleon's *coup d'état*

As if to confirm this, a new 'king' emerged from the ranks of the army – a Corsican general called Napoleon Bonaparte. He staged the first military *coup d'état* (ouster) of modern times against the collective that had ruled since the Terror. Like Julius Caesar he refused the actual crown. But his sensitivity to republican qualms was a sham – he was already a dictator and in 1804 declared himself emperor. Under Napoleon there were no longer any illusions about exporting revolution: his wars were for the greater glory of himself and France. He conquered most of Italy and Spain, bested Prussia and Austria and spent a decade threatening to rule the whole of Europe. He was finally defeated by his own egocentric ambition when he attacked Russia – the Russians and their winter eventually crushed his invasionary force in 1812. Rebellions then sprang up against the French everywhere and he was forced to abdicate in 1814. The following year Napoleon returned from exile to launch another campaign but was crushed by Belgian, British and Prussian forces at Waterloo in Belgium.

1815 – Rent-a-king

So the great popular forces unleashed by the French Revolution had a dismal end, subjugated and misused at the hands of a yet another self-important autocrat. The old regimes of Europe closed ranks and tried to pretend nothing had happened and at the Congress of Vienna in 1815 they had the first meeting of 'superpowers' to divide up their world as they thought fit.

Monarchy was their universal panacea. The memory and threat of republicanism was to be expunged from every part of Europe. Republican Holland was forced to unite with Belgium under one king; Sweden and Norway were yoked together; Poland and Italy were carved up between the Great Powers. In France a king was reinstated and when the Spanish people opposed their own monarchy their rebellion was put down by a French army with the approval of the rest of Europe.

This collusion of monarchs went so far that Austria even suggested raising a European army to fight on behalf of the Spanish Crown against Bolívar's anti-colonial armies in Latin America. They were only stopped by the promise of US President Monroe in 1823 that any European intervention in the Americas would be seen as a hostile act, a doctrine which helped the New World to remain aloof from European power politics for the next century.

Each of the restored monarchs set about turning

back the clock to absolutism and privilege. But they didn't have it all their own way. The French king overdid the financial compensation to the aristocracy and was deposed by another Paris uprising in 1830. This time the Parisians had less lofty ambitions and a milder, constitutional monarchy was established. There were republican rebellions (also in 1830) in Poland, Italy and Germany. A Belgian struggle for independence resulted in their having a German king foisted on them, a fate which had already befallen republican Greece the year before. Germany, in those crazy days, seemed to offer a rent-a-king service to the rest of Europe – which explains why almost every European royal family in the 20th century was still closely related to each other.

15 Revolution

The industrial juggernaut gathers speed. A working class is twisted into shape by hellish conditions in factories and slums – and new socialist ideas give it some hope.

THE WORLD WOULD never be the same. Conservatives and liberals had battled their ways to new societies in Europe and the Americas. But there was another revolution which doomed the arthritic political structures of the old world: science.

Scientific research had already helped vastly increase food production during the 18th century by means of fertilizer and new machinery. But metallurgy would be the branch of science with the greatest overall impact. This had not advanced since the discovery of iron 5,000 years earlier but now iron could be rolled out in sheets and in turn this made the steam engine possible. Two vital new forms of transport emerged for the 19th century from Britain: the first steamboat put out on to the Firth of Clyde in 1802; and in 1804 the first locomotive was developed, to be followed by the first railway on Teesside in 1825.

This tenfold increase in travel velocity had a momentous impact. Previous journeys had been restricted to horse speed: Napoleon traveled between France and Italy at much the same rate as Caesar went from Gaul to Rome. The horse influenced political organization too: even the biggest European states are of a size comfortable for equine communication. In the US, however, the availability of the railways drew a different political map. Trains could streak across the central plains to the Pacific and, together with the telegraph, allow a single government (and a single homogenous culture) to embrace a huge territory.

1830 – Satanic mills

But the costs and benefits of the new technology were

unequally shared. With the demise of the countryside economy rural families were forced into the sprawling, filthy streets of the new cities to seek badly paid work in appalling conditions. For these people the benefits of the Industrial Revolution hardly exceeded its costs.

Peasant communities might have found life hard but it was at least natural and comprehensible and women and men could often work in partnership. But in the cities they faced long working days which were a mental as well as physical torture. And they were likely to acquire lung diseases at work and other infections in their intolerable home conditions. Factory owners had complete power over their own workforce; Engels noted that factory women had no right to refuse the owner's sexual advances. And even the sustaining sense of partnership at home was

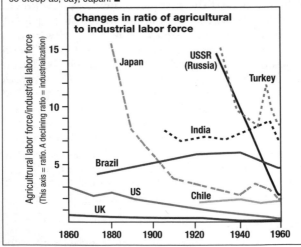

From fields to factories (1860-1960)

As countries industrialized, workers moved away from agriculture into industry. In 1930, in most African countries, farming absorbed over 80% of the work force; whereas in Europe the figure was around 40%. The US and UK had already industrialized by 1860, so their curves are not so steep as, say, Japan. ∎

Changes in ratio of agricultural to industrial labor force

Agricultrural labor force/industrial labor force
(This axis = ratio. A declining ratio = industrialization)

Japan

USSR (Russia)

Turkey

India

Brazil

US

Chile

UK

1860 1880 1900 1920 1940 1960

Third World Atlas, Open University 1994

undermined: men and women worked separately with unequal pay and there arose the concept of the male breadwinner (from which we have still not entirely recovered).

1848 – Working-class politics

All this gave a spur to the radical political thinking that the French Revolution had released throughout Europe. People thrown together in the cities acquired a sense of solidarity in their plight which they could never have conceived in thousands of fragmented farming villages. The working class realized that it was an oppressed mass at the bottom of society.

Education also helped to spread radical ideas. People had to learn enough at least to be able to control the new machines. And this was largely why mass education was introduced during the 19th century. It was primarily due not to philanthropy or Christian charity (though these doubtless played their part) but to the needs of capitalism. But now ordinary people could read about the new political ideas of socialism, communism or simple social justice. And they responded throughout mid-19th-century Europe with occasional rebellions against the appalling inequalities and living conditions of the Industrial Revolution.

Chartism was the first real working-class political movement in Britain. Between 1838 and 1848 it agitated for the universal vote (though only for men) and a general improvement of conditions. But there was no revolution in Britain, despite the massive unrest among the new industrial workers – perhaps because the middle class had been satisfied by modest electoral reform in 1832.

In the rest of Europe the liberal middle classes staged revolutions. The French deposed another king in 1848 and this time a republic was established for good; the news spread by telegraph across Europe sparking off rebellions against the outdated old order in Vienna, Rome, Milan and most German cities.

The new politics of the working class was given intellectual shape by the writings of two Germans living in England: Karl Marx and Friedrich Engels. They believed that when the working class eventually learned more about the structure of society and became fully conscious of its own oppression, it would seize power and property for the common good. Their Communist Manifesto gave momentum to the new idea of socialism.

But this frightened rather than inspired the rebellious middle-class liberals of Europe. They feared that if the working class gained political power this would threaten middle-class property. So they chose instead to compromise with the old regimes provided they were given a voice in parliament. This settlement was played out right across Europe. From now on revolution was to be the province of the working class.

1850-1914 – Industrial energy

Meanwhile the industrial juggernaut gathered momentum. The potential wealth of the US was being realized. Vast amounts of wheat, cotton and tobacco were produced for export, and a domestic market swelling all the time with new immigrants from Europe (4.5 million between 1841 and 1860) was guaranteeing prosperity. Britain had been the industrial pioneer, but its factories had been built for coal and steam. Its competitors could adapt to newer forms of energy: the Germans perfected electric dynamos in the 1860s and the internal combustion engine in the 1870s; oil itself became available from 1858 onwards after its discovery in the US state of Pennsylvania. As a result, the newer industrial economies of Germany and the US powered ahead, fueled also by their larger populations. Whereas British industrial output doubled between 1870 and 1914, US output tripled and German quadrupled.

Private banking systems were being established in

every country from 1850 onwards. And there were even international banking houses like the Rothschilds. Banks began to offer loans to middle-class people to buy their own property. The British pound and the French franc became accepted as units of exchange all over the world. And big industrial companies began to take over smaller ones to reduce costs – by 1905 Standard Oil controlled 85 per cent of US oil production and 95 per cent of all international oil trade.

1860-1914 – Industrialized leisure
The Industrial Revolution transformed the lives of ordinary people in the West. In the 1860s the majority of people in the US and Western Europe lived in villages; by 1914 the majority lived in cities. The change was most marked of all in England, where by 1900 only 10 per cent of the workforce lived in rural areas.

Despite the overcrowded slums and appalling working conditions, the quality of life improved in some ways. Primary schooling for girls and boys was near universal in the Northeast and Midwest of the US by the middle of the 19th century; Britain made primary education compulsory in 1870 and France in 1882. And the growth of trade unions also eventually improved working conditions.

Mass production had made food cheaper – a loaf of bread in Britain in 1904 was a quarter of its 1870 price. So for the first time even the working class had some money left over to spend on leisure. This was the era in which daily newspapers sprang up, when popular theater and music halls boomed, and when people began to relish the new mobility given them by the bicycle. The majority of people's lives in Western countries were beginning to resemble our own more closely.

16 Carving up the world

Imperial arrogance reaches new heights and white settlers massacre more native people in the colonies. European rulers divide the 'magnificent African cake' between them. But they are shocked to their racist boots when an Asian people learns the same industrial and military tricks – and does them much better.

EUROPEANS AND NORTH AMERICANS dominated 35 per cent of the world's land surface in 1800 and had little interest in expanding any further. Yet by 1914 they were to control 84 per cent. This change of heart was caused by the Industrial Revolution and its demands for minerals and other natural resources. Overseas colonies came to be seen as huge mines and plantations which no self-respecting industrializing country could be without.

1788 – Australian genocide

Britain's settlements in Canada and Australia had often been considered more trouble than they were worth. But the new transport technology transformed Canada's fortunes. Not only could the country now spread right across the continent but its farmers could also market their produce in Europe. There remained dissent, though, between French and British inhabitants which was only defused by a new federal constitution in 1867.

Australia had been seen as little more than a dumping ground for convicts. But it was being cleared nevertheless of its 500 Aboriginal nations. It has suited some white Australians to paint Aboriginals as an entirely primitive people, who had developed no settled housing or agriculture of any sort in thousands of years of independence (not unlike the way Europeans denied African cultural achievements). And it is true that in desert regions the Aboriginals were nomadic hunting and gathering people – they could not have survived any other way. But in the more fertile areas, they built villages, grew root crops and controlled pasture animals.

These settled people were the first to be dispossessed and massacred when British convicts started to arrive in 1788 – since they occupied the most attractive land. Even the British Parliament in 1837 declared itself appalled by what was happening to Aboriginals, who had been 'treated as thieves and robbers' and 'driven back into the interior as if they were dogs or kangaroos'. This was inaccurate: more often than not Aboriginals were killed rather than required to move on. In Tasmania, for instance, most of the original inhabitants were murdered between 1804 and 1834 and rewards were offered for every Aboriginal captured. Later in the century a racist pseudo-science led many whites to see such murder as a duty: 'we invoke and remorselessly fulfill the inexorable law of natural selection when exterminating the inferior Australian'. The British Commissioner in 1883 reported: 'I have heard men of culture and refinement, of the greatest humanity and kindness to their fellow whites... talk, not only of the wholesale butchery... but of the individual murder of natives, exactly as they would talk of a day's sport, or of having to kill some troublesome animal'.

By this time the colony was greatly valued in Britain, a change in attitude not unconnected with the discovery of copper in 1842 and of gold seven years later, but also the importance of wool to the industrial factories.

1840 – Maori wars

Maori people probably settled the islands they called Aotearoa after an epic voyage from Tahiti some time before AD 900. These were by far the biggest islands in the South Pacific, yet Europeans steered well clear, partly because of a climate which was wet and unattractive in comparison with other Pacific islands but also because of the Maori people's fierce response to attempted landings.

The first permanent white settlers of what they called New Zealand in 1814 were missionaries. But they caused much more damage at first by trading guns for food than by imposing their religion – they didn't make a single convert for the first 11 years. A local chief persuaded them to send him to London, where he was showered with gifts by polite society. Passing through Sydney on the way home he traded these gifts for hundreds of muskets, not for use against the settlers (who seemed no threat), but against other Maori. At least 25 per cent of the 150,000 population died in appalling ethnic wars which ensued between 1821 and 1840.

By this time Maori hostility to foreigners had been transformed into a great enthusiasm for trading. Many deserted their healthy villages in the hills in order to work for the settlers in the coastal areas. Here, however, they were more susceptible to the alien diseases brought in on the ships – a problem exacerbated by missionaries' attempts to persuade Maori people to cover themselves with blankets. This caught on as a status symbol and people began to wear as many as possible in all weathers and no matter how dirty they became. As much due to this as to their own wars, the Maori population began to decline markedly.

There were still only a thousand British settlers in 1838 but in 1840 Britain formally annexed New Zealand and concluded the Treaty of Waitangi, which Maori people thought would guarantee them control over their own lands. But it proved no protection against the land hunger of the newcomers and a protracted, though not particularly bloody, war ensued. As in so many of the clashes between Europeans and native peoples, a different conception of land was at the heart of the problem. Maori people regarded land as held in perpetual trust for all

Pacific paradise lost

The Pacific islands were originally colonized by waves of migration from Asia over many thousands of years. People of many different racial types had colonized the islands closest to Asia – modern Melanesia – by 2,000 BC. And another wave of settlers reached the next most accessible group – known now as Micronesia – around 1,500 BC.

But to reach the islands further away – Polynesia – required seafaring skill, a spirit of adventure and great powers of endurance. These epic voyages took place between AD 100 and 1000 in sturdy boats which had to carry not only 10 or 15 people but also enough animals, food supplies and water to sustain them on the journey and help them to build a life when they struck land. What can have driven these people to set out across thousands of miles of open sea without navigational aids or any idea whether there was land at the other end? Famine? A fearsome conqueror? We are unlikely ever to know.

The Polynesians developed all kinds of different societies – and not all were paradises free from war or cruelty. The people of Easter Island have aroused great interest because of the huge megalithic stone images of their chiefs. They were also the only Pacific people to use writing (their script was a mirror image of that from the first Indian civilization, the Harappans, though it is uncertain how this came about). But their culture seems to have revolved around war, perhaps because natural resources were limited on this relatively barren island. Just as common as the megaliths are the small figurines which show people suffering from the most extreme starvation. Another people, the Tongans, evolved what might be the most aggressively unequal society in history. No two Tongan people could have the same status; all ordinary women were at the disposal of the male aristocracy; commoners were arbitrarily beaten up or killed and could look forward only to extinction – in contrast to the afterlife of feasting enjoyed by the upper class.

But these were extremes and life for many Pacific islanders before the Europeans arrived would have been quite as idyllic as the conventional image; they could gather plenty of food and didn't need to work to survive. The first European contact set the pattern for what was to come. Ferdinand Magellan (one of whose Portuguese ships was to be the first to make it around the world) landed at Guam in Micronesia in 1519. The Portuguese burned down 50 houses and killed seven people when islanders stole a boat.

It was not until the 18th century that sailors seriously explored the islands. They were hardly Europe's best ambassadors. Their voyages had been long and arduous and the Pacific islanders provided opportunities for the diversions of sex and violence. Island cultures which had developed a healthily free attitude to sexual pleasure found themselves blighted by the European gift of venereal disease.

By 1912 all the major islands had been claimed by one or other of the Western powers. ∎

members of their group; the British could not understand anything but private ownership and frequently bought titles from people who had no rights to them in the first place. The war gave the settlers the excuse to confiscate over 7,000 square miles (18,000 square kilometers) and a law was passed which enforced the private ownership of land.

Maori people could not resist the tide, especially after gold was discovered in 1864. And the white population quadrupled in three years to reach 219,000, while Maori people were threatened with extinction, having declined to 38,500. The universal assumption among white New Zealanders by now was that Maori people would disappear within a few years, which puts a rather cynical gloss on their granting them the vote in 1867. But they did not die out, probably because an economic depression hit the colony towards the end of the century and reduced the pressure on the little land they had left.

1652-1910 South Africa

South Africa was the other significant white colony. Its coastal region had been claimed by Dutch settlers in 1652, who had soon reduced the hunter-gathering Khoisan inhabitants of the Cape to subjection. By the 1770s they were pushing deeper into the interior and encountering much more developed African peoples, with a thousand years of political history behind them. There followed a century of intermittent wars in which Xhosa, Zulu, Sotho and other groups resisted the white settlers, many of whom were by that time British as well as Dutch.

When the British gained power in the Cape they outlawed slavery – in line with new thinking from home. This led the dissatisfied Dutch (or Boers) to set out on their Great Trek north in 1836 and eventually establish separate republics in the (then) Transvaal and Orange Free State. Earlier, a Zulu warrior called Shaka (who died in 1828) had militarized his army to great effect and built a great empire in what is now KwaZulu-Natal. But the British could not bear to see an independent black state under their noses and invaded with a small force in 1879, only to be routed by the Zulu army under one of Shaka's successors, Cetshwayo. New troops with the latest technology in machine guns were brought from Britain to avenge this affront to imperial dignity and Zulu independence was crushed.

The British then picked a quarrel with the Boers so as to get their hands on the gold that had been discovered in the Transvaal – and had their way after a bitter three-year war in 1902. The independent union of South Africa was founded in 1910 based on rule by both groups of white settlers. Its new laws systematized anti-black discrimination in every area of life and awarded 90 per cent of the land to white owners, leaving the other 10 per cent as 'Native Reserves' for the black majority. The full-blown doctrine of apartheid by which South Africa oppressed its own people and degraded the international community was not to be introduced until 1948, but the legal framework of racism was in place from 1910.

1878 – Scramble for Africa

Until the second half of the 19th century, Europeans only wanted foreign lands which offered precious metals, spices or slaves. But new industries were now calling out for tropical raw materials such as palm oil and rubber. So national flags were planted in every corner of the globe that might prove advantageous – particularly in Africa.

The explorers arrived first and drew the maps; the missionaries and the soldiers followed. Africans fought back almost everywhere and initially had some success – but once the new machine guns arrived from Europe, they had no real answer. And almost as effective as the Gatling and Maxim guns was the invincible racist arrogance of the Europeans who had persuaded themselves that it was in Africans' own long-term interests to be murdered and subjected. Kipling summed it up in a famous poem: '*Take up the White Man's burden/Send forth the best ye breed/Go, bind you sons in exile/To serve your captives' need;/To wait in heavy harness/On fluttered folk and wild,/Your new-caught, sullen peoples/Half-devil and half-child.*'

By the end of the century the continent's only role seemed to be to channel raw materials back to Europe. The colonial powers drew maps with arbitrary borders which took no account of local geography, tribal distribution or language. Only two African countries remained independent: Abyssinia (later Ethiopia), which defeated an Italian attempt to colonize it at the Battle of Adowa in 1896; and Liberia, a country established for liberated American slaves.

1857 – Indian Mutiny

Recent developments in technology had convinced Europeans that they were innately superior – even to those peoples of Asia who, for centuries, had enjoyed cultures of immense sophistication.

With this kind of arrogance Britain's East India Company had gained control of most of the subcontinent. But in 1857 the Company's Indian troops mutinied. The rebellion quickly spread to the domains of all the princes and landowners in the north who resented the British, and was only suppressed after 14 months of bitter fighting – one of the first wars of liberation fought by a black nation against white colonial power. After the Mutiny, India was annexed by the British Crown and direct rule under a Viceroy began; in 1877 Queen Victoria was declared Empress of India.

1842-1911 Revolution in China

The Chinese fought numerous brief and brutish wars in the mid-19th century aimed at stamping out the drug trafficking of the British who were shipping in opium from India. They needed to break the habit – opium was dislocating the economy by replacing silver as the main form of exchange. But they failed and lost Hong Kong to boot. The Ch'ing dynasty also had internal political problems. Widespread unrest in the 1850s culminated in virtual civil war, as a rebel army one million strong captured Nanking in 1853 and threatened both Peking and Shanghai. The rebellion was put down in 1864 but left as many as 20 million dead and the Ch'ing dynasty was never as secure afterwards.

It was certainly not strong enough to ward off the predatory Europeans. An Anglo-French army marched on Peking in 1860 to secure more trading concessions; the French occupied Indo-China and in Burma the British put down roots. By 1900 all the 'Great Powers' were anxious for a slice of the action. Not surprisingly there was an anti-European popular protest in Peking (the 'Boxer Rebellion') which the Ch'ing rulers momentarily encouraged. It was put down by allied Western troops who rescued their diplomats but also stole much valuable property. The Russians then seized Manchuria and the British invaded Tibet. This humiliation for China eventually had some kind of long-term benefit when the last emperor was consigned to history by a rebellion in 1911. A new Nationalist government under Sun Yat-sen came to power in Peking with the belief that China should now modernize to compete with the West. But its power was very limited: most of the country was yet again racked by divisions, with semi-independent states ruled by local warlords.

1853-1914 Japan joins the game

It was Japan which demonstrated for all time that Europeans had no monopoly on intelligence, industrial advantage or military strength. Two centuries of self-imposed isolation ended in 1853 when four US warships arrived demanding that Japan open up to trade; 12 years later the Europeans joined them and, by sheer naval force, imposed trading treaties which would allow Western exploitation to begin.

But for once it didn't work. Humiliated by its 'shameful inferiority' to the West, Japan's response was to launch itself into fundamental change. The shoguns – who had for centuries ruled as an institutionalized military dictatorship – were pushed aside in 1868 by the Emperor in the Meiji Restoration. Ironically this reassertion of Japanese traditions was also the quickest and most effective route to revolutionary renewal as the country threw itself into learning all the industrial secrets of the modern world. And by the end of the century – within just one generation – it had done this so effectively that it was accepted as an equal by Britain and the US. Feudalism was abolished in 1871; a national education system established in 1872; a conscript army was created in 1873; and during the ensuing decades its factories were so productive that exports soared from 30 million yen in 1878-82 to 932 million yen in 1913-17. The myth of Western superiority should have been utterly shattered. Sadly, it still bedevils us, with the Japanese admitted to an élite club as the exceptions that somehow prove the rule.

But for some European powers, the lesson could only be learned militarily. Czarist Russia continued its program of conquest and adventure in Asia. Japan waited until it considered that its fleet and its army were up to the task and then roundly defeated the Russians on both land and sea. In 1905 the Czar was forced to withdraw, not least because this futile and ridiculous war had provoked an attempted revolution at home.

17 Total war

The European powers show no sign of living up to their claim to be 'civilized'. Not content with competing industrially, they channel their ingenuity into the manufacture of ever better weapons. The First World War is the inevitable result.

MUCH OF EUROPE'S energy in the second half of the 19th century was expended on internecine fighting. One important consequence of these wars (the details of which are not that significant) was the emergence of Italy and Germany as unified countries – previously they had been collections of small states. And Germany united under the Prussian king (who became the emperor or Kaiser) became Europe's most powerful nation.

These new powers were frustrated by their inability to exploit the new communications technology in the way that the US could. Their borders now seemed ridiculously small for a nation-state. Britain had its vast empire to play around in; and Russia was able to expand eastwards unchallenged but for scattered nomadic peoples – its railway across Siberia finally reached the Pacific in 1905, a distance of 4,600 miles (7,360 kilometers). But the other European countries had nowhere to go.

They held, however, not a new ideal of co-operation but rather the tired old dream of Charlemagne and Napoleon, of one power conquering all the others. Germany was in the best position to achieve this.

1914 – First World War
War was inevitable. The only surprise was that it took until 1914 to break out. Germany, Austria and Turkey were ranged against France, Belgium, Russia, Britain and Serbia. Other independent countries – Japan, the US and China – later joined the alliance against Germany. But the colonies were involved too.

Total war

Thousands of men – Indians and Kenyans, Canadians and Australians – were forced to risk their lives for the petty pride of a colonial master. This is why the 1914-18 conflict can legitimately be called the First World War.

This war has become synonymous with the futile waste of human life. When the initial offensives (the Germans against France and the Russians against Germany) had been beaten back, the War settled into an appalling stalemate. Armies of millions faced each other, with their front lines set in trenches no more than a few hundred yards/meters apart.

The old military thinking – still locked into a musket-and-cavalry-charge mentality – was quite incapable of dealing with the changed world. The soldiers themselves – most of them, at least in the early years, volunteers drawn into danger out of misguided notions of patriotic or Christian duty – experienced unimaginably bad living conditions, subject to the bleak weather of Northern Europe, to the reckless eccentricities of their upper-class commanders and to the first appearance of poison gas, the most terrifyingly inhumane weapon history had yet seen. If they survived, it was often without parts of their bodies and just as often without parts of their minds. Humanity, as so often, had proved unable to cope with the technological knowledge it had garnered.

1918 – The home fires burn
Soldiers were not the only victims. Wars have regularly devastated whole communities: cities have been plundered, women raped and innocents put to the sword. But this war had an impact way beyond the muddy battlefields. With so many young men called up into military service, women and old people were recruited for factories and farms. And they too were vulnerable to attack as the new airplanes (these had appeared in 1909) and inflatable airships carried bombs deep beyond enemy lines. Battles could no longer be fought by gentlemen's agreement at an appointed time and place. The concept of total war had arrived.

Votes for women

The First World War had one positive spin-off: women won the vote. This was difficult for male leaders to deny any longer when women had demonstrated that they were the equals of men as industrial and agricultural workers – by 1916 1.6 million women had been working in Britain, half of them in engineering plants.

But they had ingrained prejudice to overcome. Darwin had dismissed the female brain as less highly evolved; doctors had seen all women as naturally weaker and potential invalids. Education was said to threaten women's sanity or even, according to one 'philosopher', to produce flat chests.

Women were outraged by such idiocies and began to campaign for their rights in the mid-19th century. Being denied the vote seemed the ultimate indignity. Britain's electoral reform of 1832 gave more men the vote but specifically excluded women (though abbesses had previously sat in parliament).

British women at the 1840 world anti-slavery congress spread the word to their American sisters; in 1869 Elizabeth Cady Stanton and Susan B Anthony launched the US feminist newsletter *Revolution* and the state of Wyoming became the first to offer women the vote. The first country – New Zealand – was not to follow suit until 1893 and in too many cases women had to wait until after the War for their formal emancipation.

Winning the vote was a great achievement. But the political results of the victory were disappointing: early feminists had hoped it would lead to a greater social and economic equality with men. Instead women in the 20th century demonstrated a different kind of equality by voting in much the same way as men, which made the march towards women's rights a painfully slow one. The vote was not enough. ∎

By 1918 the whole of Europe and much of the world beyond was exhausted by this catastrophe. Famine was widespread – food supplies had been cut by the disruption of farming and the conscription of peasants. And an influenza epidemic worldwide killed even more millions than were killed directly by the War.

The War wasn't won in the end. It collapsed. Germany's official defeat, however, was largely because one million US troops joined the fray in the final year. At least eight million people had died.

18 The power of the workers

The Russian people depose a Czar and then launch into the world's first experiment in worker power. They survive under siege but the Revolution is hijacked by the ruthless dictator Stalin – a blow from which the Left worldwide has still not recovered.

THE RUSSIAN REVOLUTION of 1917 was the first in history to take power in the name and interests of peasant and working-class people.

Czarist Russia, with its absolute monarchy and extraordinary inequality, was a hangover from the days before the French Revolution. Peasant communities made up most of the country. And they might have continued stoically to endure this archaic regime had it not been for the First World War. By 1917 hundreds of thousands of peasant conscripts had lost their lives responding to repeated calls to perform their duty to country and Czar – and their communities were reaching the limits of compliance.

In the army they were thrown together with workers from the new factories in the cities. And the two groups made common cause, building up a disgust for the system that had led them into this mess. In March 1917 food riots in Petrograd (now St Petersburg) turned into insurrection; the response was so general and widespread that the Czar was forced to abdicate. A reformist republican government was established. It attempted to carry on the war but could satisfy neither its allies nor the increasingly radical demands for social change. The army rebelled after another disastrous offensive and the Communists under Vladimir Ilyich Ulyanov – better known by his underground alias of Lenin – seized power. They called themselves Bolsheviks – the 'majority'.

1917 – Land and wealth distributed
The Bolsheviks embarked almost immediately upon

the most profoundly radical political and social experiment in history. Using the ideas of Karl Marx they aimed to create an entirely new society. The very day after seizing power, they announced that all landed estates should be redistributed to the peasants, all banks nationalized and private accounts confiscated. Then they gave workers control over factories, confiscated all church property and repudiated the national debt. But their task was made impossible in the early years by the hostility of every other nation in Europe. Terrified by the possibility that the Bolshevik 'disease' might spread to their own countries, they tried to destabilize the new regime in any way they could. The Russian people found themselves attacked not only by anti-Bolshevik Russians but also by Britain, France, Japan, Estonia and Poland.

The Bolsheviks survived – largely because the mass of people were behind them – but their attempts at revolutionary change were in tatters by 1921: agricultural production had collapsed so that the towns and cities went hungry; industrial production was not in much better shape; and drought caused a famine in which millions of peasants died. Faced with this crisis, Lenin marked time by permitting some private enterprise and it was only after his death that the policy changed. Stalin then took over (after a battle with Trotsky for the succession) and in 1928 launched into the full collectivization of industry and agriculture which was to lay the groundwork for the Soviet Union's next half-century.

The State was to control everything, from production quotas to newspapers and political ideas. This worked well enough on the industrial side and sparked off remarkable improvements in public health and life expectancy. But the agricultural policies were disastrous. By 1934 some 200,000 large collective farms had been created, to the disappointment of poorer peasants who had hoped that the Revolution might give them their own plot of land. The more prosperous peasants (the *kulaks*) were even more vigorously opposed to this and many thousands were either killed or sent to Siberian labor camps for 're-education'.

1935 – Stalin's Terror
This concentration of power in the center was dangerous not least because it put more and more control in the hands of Stalin himself. He became paranoically obsessed with his own power and survival. One by one all potential opponents, including all the original Bolshevik leaders, were killed off; far worse, millions of Soviet citizens were arrested in 'purges' between 1935 and 1939 – no-one knows how many of them died, either by execution or in Siberian labor camps, but it probably also ran into millions. Even ordinary people unaffected by the purges had to live in constant fear of offending the new orthodoxy, the Party machine. Stalin was a brutal tyrant – as cruel and as uncaring of the needs of ordinary people as any Czar, Ivan the Terrible included. But his tyranny was the greater because it was expressed through a totalitarian state which aimed to control not just the economic or the political spheres but also people's words and feelings, their very sense of truth. And by doing all this in the name of socialism, of the honorable ideas of Marx, Stalin set back the cause of the Left worldwide. It has still not recovered.

19 Capitalism and Fascism

International government is attempted and fails miserably. Western capitalism goes on a spending spree – but it collapses violently and the poor pay the price. Fascism's brutal remedies have popular appeal and bring the world to war again.

THE WAR TO end all wars. That at least was how the Western governments saw the First World War. Now they could lay the plans for a new and peaceful world. A League of Nations was set up in a foreshadowing of today's United Nations and there seemed some hope that the good sense of internationalism would prevail. The colonized countries, in particular, hoped that the League of Nations would help them reach independence.

But the League had no real power and was in any case dominated by Britain and France (the US Congress refused to join and the Soviet Union was not allowed to do so). And, far from overseeing a retreat from colonialism, the League of Nations actually bolstered it by redistributing the ex-German and Turkish colonies under the guise of League 'mandates'.

It was as if nothing had been learned from the War. Government planning which had been essential in wartime and had helped pull nations together, was discarded. Industrialists were encouraged to make as much money as they could and the old privileges were reasserted. Ordinary people who had fought in the trenches, or run the factories, were expected to forget the promises of a better world and resume their rightful place at the bottom of the heap.

Such people were even worse off in Germany which was having to pay massive amounts in reparations to the Allies. There was enormous social unrest. Indeed immediately after the War and the abdication of the Kaiser, visionary activists such as Rosa Luxemburg almost inspired a socialist revolution. But the revolt in Berlin was put down by the army on behalf of a group of liberal parliamentarians and all the leading socialists were either killed or imprisoned. The Weimar Republic (named after the city where it was declared) set out on its shaky path through the 1920s – printing money to pay its debts. Germany was not the only country stoking up inflation but it was certainly the most spectacular example – the dollar was worth 50 marks in 1922 and 2.5 trillion marks in 1924.

1920s – capitalism's house of cards
Elsewhere in the West in the 1920s the people who had money were speculating as if there were no tomorrow. Everything was being left to the market and the devil take the hindmost. Few governments were sensibly planning their nations' affairs and there were signs of dangerous fracture and disintegration in most of the powerful economies. Gangsterism flourished in the US after the prohibition of alcohol and was indicative of the general social climate.

A different and even more dangerous kind of gangsterism won political power in Italy. Socialists there inspired by the Russian Revolution had produced a wave of strikes. The capitalists (particularly the Fiat and Pirelli companies) were terrified by the prospect of revolution and invested money and support in Benito Mussolini and his Fascists. In fact the Fascists (the word was taken from the *fasces*, a ancient Roman symbol of authority) were little more than a private army of thugs who beat up socialists and broke up strikes. A general strike in 1922 brought Mussolini to the brink of leading a coup; instead he was invited into power by the King and thereafter any pretense at democracy vanished. There were similar stirrings on the far Right in Germany.

1929 – Wall Street Crash
The optimism of the rich – and contempt for the

Why Africans go hungry

Europeans saw their tropical dependencies as mere suppliers of raw materials. This is why farmers in Mozambique and Angola, for instance, were forced to stop growing food for local people and start growing cotton to feed the textile industry in Portugal.

The farmers received very little for the raw cotton (prices were set artificially low by the colonial administration) and often found themselves buying it back from Portugal as clothing at artificially high prices.

This was by no means unique to the Portuguese. Despite all the rhetoric about civilizing and educating the natives, every European power treated its colonies in much the same manner – as a way of transferring wealth from Africa to Europe. Areas that were fertile or rich in mineral deposits would be exploited for all they were worth and settled by Europeans. The vast tracts which did not have such natural advantages would receive few of the colonial 'benefits' in the shape of schools or clinics but would be expected to offer their able-bodied people as migrant laborers for the plantations and mines. Yet again the fabric of African society was torn apart.

And so was its food production. The famines and widespread malnutrition in Africa today have their roots in colonial policies which forced farmers away from growing food and into cultivating cash crops that would be of use to Europeans. After the Second World War, for example, those same cotton-growing areas of Mozambique which had once been a granary for the surrounding regions became areas of famine. People the length and breadth of Africa had been guided by colonialism into the same trap – and have still not found a way out. ∎

needs of the poor – which characterized the 1920s came to an abrupt end in October 1929 when the financial house of cards in the US came tumbling down. Share prices plummeted and banks collapsed. The US economy plunged into deep recession, partly because it had been so thoroughly based on catering to the needs of the rich. Had industry been producing more basic items for mass consumption, demand could not have fallen by much but the market for sailing boats and luxuries was extinguished overnight.

Factories closed down and farmers went bankrupt; unemployment soared and starvation threatened. And there were disastrous knock-on effects throughout the world. International trade slumped by 60 per cent and industrial production by 40 per cent. Unemployment soared to 40 per cent of the workforce in Germany by 1930; and in the US and Britain in 1933 it approached 25 per cent.

1930s – Right-wing reaction

The world was in crisis. Established governments were blamed and sacked. In Spain the King was replaced by a republican government; and in Mexico the new

China's revolution

In China a charismatic but ruthless leader was emerging in the 1920s at the same time as Fascism was on the rise in Europe. The 1911 Revolution, which had ousted the last emperor, had not managed to hold the country together. Warlords vied for control of their own regions. The Revolution had started with three principles – nationalism, democracy and social justice. But only the first seemed much in evidence, especially after Sun Yat-sen died and was replaced by his general, Chiang Kai-shek.

Chiang's forces reunified China in 1926 with the help of the newly founded Communist Party and removed the power of the local warlords. But he then turned on his Communist allies, defeating them after a long civil war. The Communist survivors avoided capture by marching right across the mountainous central part of China in 1934. They seemed unlikely to pose any further threat. But the Long March became a potent symbol as the Communist leader, Mao Zedong, formulated his new idea of a Marxist revolution based on the peasants rather than the industrial working class.

The Japanese invasion of China in 1937 forced the Nationalists and Communists into a Popular Front to defend the country. But by the end of their 10-year alliance, Communist strength had grown from 30,000 to almost three million. City after city fell to the Red Army and Mao Zedong proclaimed the new People's Republic in 1949.

The Maoist Revolution marked a break with the thousands of years of inequality presided over by the emperors. It did the impossible, dragging almost a quarter of the world's population out of a past which had been punctuated continually by famine and civil war. Life expectancy figures tell their own story: before the Revolution, people could only expect to live 36 years; by 1960 this had climbed to 47 and by 1975 to 65. Mao's dictatorial social engineering had its disastrous effects too – an estimated 20 million died in the famine caused by his Great Leap Forward (the collectivization of agriculture) in 1959. And the political repression of the Mao years has carried through into China's post-Maoist era. But the Chinese Revolution still deserves to be seen as a fantastic achievement. ■

president Lázaro Cárdenas pushed through some land reform, the first radical fruit of the country's 1914 revolution. In the US itself the Democrats under Franklin Roosevelt replaced the conservative Republicans. They at least had some kind of vision of what government action could do for the underprivileged (and they also put a temporary stop to the consistent US intervention in Latin America). But everywhere else the consequences of the Wall Street Crash and the Great Depression were reactionary. In Japan the militarists killed off their opponents and consolidated power; and in a host of countries in Europe and Latin America, parliaments were replaced by demagogic dictators.

1933 – The rise of Nazism

The most important developments were in Germany, where the Nazi Party, under their charismatic Austrian-born leader Adolf Hitler, held the balance of power in the first election after the Crash in 1930. Hitler just lost the presidential election two years later but was offered the Chancellorship in 1933, having been bankrolled by wealthy German industrialists who shared his obsessional hatred of Jews and communists. But they soon lost control of him and his brown- and black-shirted private armies. In 1934 Hitler assumed absolute power, banned trade unions and other parties and put all news media, universities, schools and professions under strict Nazi control.

Order of a kind was restored – the trains ran on time – and Hitler's rigid central planning was initially worthy of Stalin. He brought inflation under control and used public work schemes to get the economy back to some semblance of normality. But he had military ambitions too and in 1935 he began conscription and rearmament, flouting the peace terms imposed on Germany after the First World War. The Great Powers registered a mild protest but nothing more.

1930s – The Jewish Holocaust

Anyone outside the new orthodoxy was in trouble. Socialists, gays, Roma travelers and especially Jewish people were constantly harassed and lived in fear of beatings or the burning of their houses. Thousands disappeared, taken to concentration camps such as Belsen (set up from 1933) where they endured the most appalling conditions of hard labor, starvation and torture. As the 1930s progressed, the victimization of these groups intensified. Eventually Hitler set about the systematic murder of all the Jewish people in his expanding empire. For his 'Final Solution' he used extermination camps such as Auschwitz in Poland and by 1945 most of the Jews of Central Europe had been murdered – at least six million people.

There has been no shortage of savage violence in this brief history. But the Nazi extermination of the Jews is the single most dreadful episode in the whole of human history. Its cold premeditation and scientific operation rendered bankrupt any notion that human beings were making moral as well as technological progress.

1935 – Fascist expansion

The 'Axis' alliance of Germany, Italy and Japan, realized that it could get away with almost anything; the words of international law were not going to be backed up by military action. So in 1935 Italy, in an attempt to build an empire, invaded Abyssinia (now Ethiopia). This was one of only two African states not under colonial control and was a member of the League of Nations, yet the League did nothing to support it; within a few months Abyssinia was under Italian rule. Then in 1936 Japan invaded China, also in the first step towards an empire that it saw as commensurate with its powerful new economic status.

In Spain the republican Government came under attack in the same year from an army supported and supplied by Germany – the republicans had been threatening the wealth and land of the aristocracy and the Catholic Church. Spain's Western allies refused to help and the Government had to rely instead on a mixture of financial help from Russia and an army of volunteers. Most (though by no means all) of these 'International Brigades' were communists, who traveled from all corners of the world to risk their lives in a spirit of internationalism. But the Spanish fascists eventually triumphed in 1939.

The Nazi adventures became bolder: Hitler began to mix the notion of a Greater Germany in with his anti-Semitic, anti-communist, anti-homosexual rantings. This new country would comprise all German-speaking peoples and allow his pure Aryans more *lebensraum* (room to live). In 1936 they began the series of invasions – of the Rhineland, Austria, Czechoslovakia and Poland – which eventually brought about the Second World War.

World population

At the end of the Ice Age (10,000 BC) people lived by hunting and gathering; population was around 4 million. It rose to 14 million by the Bronze Age (3000 BC). As farming became more productive, population reached 170 million by the first century AD. It passed the one-billion mark in 1830 with advances in food production, sanitation and disease control. Today, world population stands at 6 billion. ∎

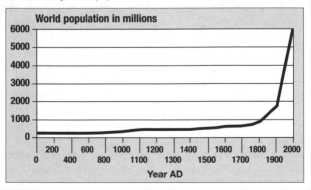

20 The radical 20th century

I AM NOT going to attempt to sum up the 60 years since the Second World War broke out using the same format as in the rest of this book. In part this is because the post-War world in all its complexity is the one the **New Internationalist** magazine reports on every month – it is also the one reflected in the other books in this *No-Nonsense Guide* series. But it is also, I admit, because I would be uncomfortable making the same kind of sweeping, broad-brushstroke assessment of the 1960s or 1980s as of the 360s.

The closer history comes to the present, the more evident the writer's bias becomes. Take any History of the World and you will find the same: it seems detached and authoritative throughout the ages until you reach the recent past. Then it's almost like a different personality takes over, one that seeks to slot recent events in world history into a particular ideological framework. Usually this is laden with right-wing value judgements: for example, a history will claim that there were no world wars after 1945 because of the mutual terror of nuclear weapons. This is not so much history as a political argument about peace and nuclear deterrence that would slot very easily into the manifestos of most conservative political parties in the West. On the other hand my own picture of recent world history would quite rightly lead you to suspect that I have a bias, too.

All historians have such a bias but they vary in their degree of readiness to advertise it, something we should be aware of as the post-millennial dust settles on the orgy of historical interpretation of 'the meaning of the 20th century'. A century, like a work of art, has as many meanings as the observer wishes to project on to it, yet few people are prepared to admit that their view is partial, that it emerges from their own personal and political agenda.

Those least prepared to own up to bias are often those with the loudest, most omnipresent voices – and they tend to see the 20th century as a battleground in which the forces of truth and light triumphed. *Time* magazine, for example, summed up it up as 'The American Century'. 'Some countries,' it said, 'base their foreign policy on realism or its Prussian-accented cousin, *realpolitik*: a cold and careful calculation of strategic interests. America is unique in that it is equally motivated by idealism. Whether it is the fight against fascism or communism, or even misconceived interventions like Vietnam, America's mission is to further not only its interests but also its values. And that idealist streak is a source of its global influence, even more than its battleships. As became clear when the Iron Curtain collapsed in 1989, America's clout in the world comes not just from its military might but from the power and appeal of its values. Which is why it did, indeed, turn out to be an American Century.'

The unshakable complacency is extraordinary. The multifarious struggles of the world's people for greater control over their own lives, for decent standards of health, education, nutrition, for social justice, for peace and civil rights, are here reduced to one central story: the ultimate victory of the particular model of democracy and capitalism patented and promoted by the United States of America.

There is another view of US foreign policy which might be thought rather closer to the mark than *Time*'s, one memorably characterized by the eminent playwright Harold Pinter as 'Do as we say – or else.'

But let's leave that by the by for the moment. We'll also leave aside that free-market capitalism and Western democracy was rescued from its direst hour in the 1940s not by the divine intervention of American troops – as implied by the opening and closing shots of Steven Spielberg's film *Saving Private Ryan* ('Old Glory' rippling in the breeze) – but rather by the Soviet Union, which could surely not have turned back the tide of Nazi Germany had it continued along Czarist or even liberal-democratic lines after its dismal experience and military performance in the First World War. It is deeply ironic that the Red Army's military success – and therefore liberal democracy's survival – probably depended on the very 'totalitarianism' that the post-War West found so abhorrent.

The important thing to recognize is that *Time* and its media allies have been hard at work representing the primary meaning of the century as residing in the victory of capitalism over communism in the Cold War between 1945 and 1990. Early in the 1990s Americans began crowing about 'the end of history' – they meant by this that the collapse of the Soviet Union had proved the inadequacy of any alternative model to capitalism, which would thereafter rule unchallenged for all eternity.

The unlikelihood of this notion will strike anyone who has even the smallest knowledge of history. Empires seem eternal when they are their height but they always contain the seeds of their own decay – and the American Empire, riven with agonizing self-doubt only two decades ago in the wake of defeat in Vietnam and President Nixon's Watergate disgrace, is nothing like as qualified to feel secure as, say, imperial Rome at the beginning of the first millennium of the Christian era.

Lessons learned and lost from three world wars

History's lessons can be vital and the Washingtonian triumphalists should have been the first to take heed of one of its lessons in particular. There were three world wars in the 20th century, two of them extremely hot and one which thankfully remained Cold. The first of those wars produced the second as certainly and inevitably as night follows day. When the terms of the Treaty of Versailles were imposed on the German losers in 1919, mainly out of the understandable bitterness and anger of the French, whose country had been occupied and ravaged out of recognition, it made an even greater whirlwind inevitable. That fact was even recognized at the time by British prime minister Lloyd George, who said the terms and reparations demanded were so harsh that 'we shall have to fight another war all over again in 25 years at three times the cost'. The economist John Maynard Keynes, meanwhile, predicted that the peace treaty would depress European economies to starvation point.

The crippling terms exacted at Versailles duly produced hyper-inflation, destroyed Germany's Weimar Republic and created the circumstances in which Hitler's vicious scapegoat-hunting ideology could flourish. And Hitler was not alone: one of the most terrifying things about journeying back through the 20th century has been to experience afresh the events of the 1930s and to see country after country fall to fascist 'strong men', whereas in my own mind's eye Fascism had always been broadly a phenomenon involving only Hitler and Mussolini.

After the Second World War the lesson had been learned and US aid via the Marshall Plan reconstructed western Europe, effectively creating the conditions for the Golden Age of economic boom in Western countries between 1950 and 1975 in which it was certainly true, in British prime minister Harold Macmillan's phrase, that people had 'never had it so good'.

But by the time the Cold War was over and it was time for the victorious West to dictate terms to a crumbling post-Communist empire, all the lessons of Versailles had been forgotten. All was triumphalism. There could be no mercy for the losers.

A system of free enterprise without controls was imposed on the new East European states and Russia the like of which had never been tried before, even at the heart of the capitalist world. The US, for all its bleating about free trade, remains instinctively protectionist. Its own response to severe economic depression in the 1930s was to invest in federal programs involving strong state intervention and the introduction of a welfare safety net under Roosevelt's New Deal. Even the fundamentalist crusade of Margaret Thatcher in Britain between 1979 and 1991 did not dismantle some of the key elements of the old welfare state.

Russia and its satellite states, however, were not to be allowed such supports – here the free market had to reign in all its magnificent implacability. Right-wing economists like Harvard's Jeffrey Sachs were sent in as consultants to ensure that the rules were followed and no soft options adopted. The glorious results of this 'peace settlement' were manifest in 1998, following the collapse of the rouble, in the sight of Russians begging for food in the streets in scenes that might have embarrassed even Czar Nicholas II. The resurgence of extremist nationalism and fascism in Russia and Eastern Europe may yet be harbingers of another whirlwind that will engulf us all.

The march of history has more than one drumbeat

History, then, is important, and the lessons of the 20th century need to be carried into the 21st rather than lost in the swirl and babble of the information age in its indefatigable pursuit of 'now'. But if the triumphalist Western version of the 20th century is one that should be challenged, what should be put in its place? There are a multitude of such histories to be written.

But, wearing my partiality on my sleeve, I will suggest that one of those alternative narratives might emphasize the place of social and political resistance in human progress. The whole notion of 'progress' is problematic, something to which I will return. But in most areas of social life in which we are sure we are 'farther on' in the year 2001 than we were in 1900, we have only advanced because people have stood up to the dominant worldview, chancing their arm and their heart in the struggle against oppression, in the aspiration for liberty or equality.

Two cases demonstrate this with absolute clarity. In 1900, the idea that all women should have the right to vote was one held only by a tiny minority considered to be on the lunatic fringe of politics. In all the world, with odd exceptions such as New Zealand/Aotearoa and the US state of Wyoming, men were complacent in their monopoly of the political process. When the battle for the vote was joined in earnest, first in Edwardian Britain, the term 'battle' was no rhetorical exaggeration. This was a campaign of a ferocity that would probably surprise people misled by sepia photographs of suffragists in prim middle-class hats and dresses. In the militant suffragist campaigns – from bombings of male politicians' country houses to vandalizations of famous paintings, from smashing the windows of public buildings to hunger strikes while in prison – there were many of the tactics of modern 'terrorism', though their targets were generally property rather than human lives.

At the beginning of the 21st century we are still far from political equality, and women's rights still need promoting and defending. But the idea of women's right of political participation has been unchallenged and unchallengeable in most of the world for decades, even if Switzerland only conceded in 1971 and the Taliban's Afghanistan has reneged today.

Something similar might be said about the idea that people of color might be capable of self-rule – an apparent absurdity in the colonial world of 1900. The notion of African liberation, in particular, had barely rippled the surface: the first Pan-African Congress was, it is true, held in London in 1900, but it had only a token presence from the African continent itself. Yet, a century later, no-one in their right minds would suggest that Africans or Indians should not rule themselves and even the bitter, long-festering wound of apartheid South Africa has at last been treated.

There is certainly a good case for saying that the

anti-colonial struggle has been far from won, that direct rule by white men in pith helmets has been traded for indirect dominion by white men in pinstripes. But the principle of self-rule, so extreme and marginal in 1900, so reviled by the powers-that-were in the India of the 1930s, the Kenya of the 1950s or the South Africa of the 1970s, is part of the established pattern of our world. The freedom-fighters and the Fenians, the terrorists and the tortured, have been eventually transmogrified into the statespeople and the saints, from Michael Collins through to Nelson Mandela.

The 'march of history' does not have only one drumbeat. At every point in the century it has been taken down side-alleys by seditionaries and run up against the barricades of dissent.

So it is that yesterday's alternative tributary becomes today's mainstream. Not by any means in all cases, since, God knows, resistance movements have no monopoly on wisdom and the catalogue of their errors and misunderstandings would itself run very long. But the need for an alternative vision of human progress and development based on social justice, equality and human rights is no less essential now than it was a century ago – and ideas that seem wild, even mad, now will be considered orthodox a further hundred years on. Our resistance and our idealism has made a difference to the 20th century – and it must make even more of a difference to the 21st.

The myth of progress

This may be an alternative narrative but it is still one which depends on the idea of progress, which any brief tour through the history of the world must at least call into question. It is salutary to read H G Wells' *A Short History of the World* now because he wrote (in 1922) at a time when it was still possible to believe that scientific progress was a wondrous force liberating us all from drudgery and want, that human development was spiraling ever onward and upward into a stratosphere of educated and civilized harmony. He could believe this only four years after the most horrific war history had yet seen because he had faith that scientific virtues would eventually overcome outdated primitive responses. It was still possible for Wells to look back over the span of history and say that it was non-stop progress (with a few hiccups here and there) from slime to fish, from apes to humans, from gathering to agriculture, from feudalism to capitalism and onwards into some kind of socialism.

Karl Marx saw things in a similar way: the process of development from feudalism through capitalism and socialism to eventual communism was historically inevitable. So too, at the opposite ideological pole, did Walt Disney. One of Disneyland Paris's more impressive exhibits today is a nine-screen cinema which shows films in the 360-degree round, so that if you see the Matterhorn in front of you, you will be able to turn your head and see Zermatt behind you as if you were truly amidst the Swiss Alps. Such setpiece scenes are woven together by an enjoyable nonsense of a narrative that has a robot time-traveler picking up 19th-century science-fiction writer Jules Verne by mistake and taking him on a journey into our own age. Naturally Verne is a sucker for the wonders of scientific progress – space rockets and racing cars – and a veil is drawn over the debit side of the ledger, such as environmental destruction. Eventually we and Verne are taken farther on into the future and are vouchsafed a brief vision of a Parisian metropolis a century or so on as a kind of science-fiction heaven on earth.

But for most of us this firm faith in scientific advancement as a guarantor of human progress is no longer so easy to retain. Science, we now realize, is not a neutral force but is harnessed to the values and power structures into which it emerges. It can be a force for bad as well as good. It has given human beings, mainly those in the white-dominated developed countries, a great deal in terms of material comfort and freedom from disease. Most inhabitants of industrialized countries, and a significant élite in developing nations, benefit from a level of ease, education and access to information undreamed of by even the most ardent optimist in 1900. But all too much of the progress has been for the exclusive benefit of the richest fifth of the world's people who now receive over 80 per cent of the world's income compared to the 2 per cent earned by the poorest fifth.

Science has, moreover, given us weapons that had us trembling on the brink of destruction for decades. The scale of devastation of human life in the last hundred years should alone be enough to dispel any lingering illusions about the inevitability of progress. Some 150 million people died in war. Around 100 million died in the great famines of the century, without even beginning to take account of those who died, quietly, deep beneath the gaze of the world's headlines, from the effects of everyday hunger and malnutrition. A further 100 million died as a result of government repression.

But it is the 14 million victims of genocide who should give us most pause. Contemplating their fate, it is easy to understand why the philosopher Isaiah Berlin said of the 20th century: 'I remember it only as the most terrible century in human history.'

All meditations on the meaning of the century, even the mainstream ones, inevitably return at this point to the Nazi Holocaust of the Jews – and the Romanies, gays and socialists who perished in the death camps alongside them. The ethnic genocide which began and ended the century – the Turkish massacre of Armenians at the beginning and the Serb 'cleansing' of Bosnians and Albanians at the end – was depressing enough evidence of the human incapacity to outgrow blind prejudice and bloodthirstiness. But the Nazi extermination program stands unique in history for its particular horror – the industrialization of mass murder, the routine annihilation of six million people by faceless bureaucrats and soldiers who were simply 'doing their job'.

A recent interview in the German magazine *Der Spiegel* with a man who worked as a doctor at Auschwitz underlines the peculiarly 20th-century horror of what Hannah Arendt called 'the banality of evil'. Dr Hans Münch conducted scientific experiments on people under the auspices of the notorious Josef Mengele. He still feels no remorse, no regrets about the part he played and he lives in comfortable retirement. 'To eradicate the Jews, that was the job of the SS at the time,' says Münch. 'I could do experiments on people, which otherwise were only possible on rabbits. It was important work for science... No, I can't say I felt pity.'

The Holocaust single-handedly demolishes the idea that the century's undoubted scientific progress was paralleled by a comparable moral progress. Even those who experienced it at first hand confess themselves unable to testify to its essential horror. 'We who survived the Camps are not true witnesses,' says the writer Primo Levi. 'We are those who, through prevarication, skill or luck, never touched bottom. Those who have, and who have seen the face of the Gorgon, did not return, or returned wordless.'

We can only hope that the Nazi Holocaust remains unparalleled in human history and that by the end of the next century the historical memory of this bleakest of episodes remains starkly alive, its lessons remembered and understood.

Earth fissures and capitalist cracks

The other force undermining the Tower of Progress at the end of the century is the destruction of the global environment. The Western industrial model which science spawned still threatens to bring the life of the planet to an abrupt end through its relentless exhaustion and pollution of natural resources. And even if enough corrections are made to our way of operating to save the earth from irreparable damage, it no longer seems possible for the 'virtues' of the Western industrial model to be exported to the whole of humanity.

Even the greatest scientific achievements seem to have their counterpoint in environmental devastation, whether the vast increases in food production which have destroyed natural habitats and rendered huge tracts of land infertile or the advantages of electricity or high-speed travel which have ultimately, through the emission of gases into the atmosphere, produced the alarming phenomenon of global warming.

Yet paradoxically, from the point of view of resistance and the search for an alternative path to the current global economic model, the environment provides hope as well as despair. For it is here that the cracks in the capitalist system yawn widest. The free market may be capable of a great number of things for which people like me do not usually give it credit, but protecting the environment is certainly not one of them. A system built on the pursuit of profit by competing companies is bound to be incapable of safeguarding the earth's natural resources. If the environment is to be protected and the exploitation of its resources controlled – and not even the most enthusiastic optimist could believe that human society could pursue current rates of economic growth throughout the next century – it will have to be ordered and regulated by the national and supranational state.

In the working out of a sustainable future – and in the resurgence of interest in regulating the free market which will go hand-in-hand with it – will come the opportunity for resistance movements to find their voice and exert their influence. The fissures in the free-market 'end-of-history' model are already opening up.

When historian Eric Hobsbawm wrote his seminal history of the 'short 20th century' in the early 1990s, he correctly identified the free-market flagellation of

Russia and Eastern Europe as a disastrous mistake and explained why the current mania for globalization and growth could not last. But he still accepted, as did everyone else, South Korea's status as an economic 'tiger,' suggesting that the uncontrolled power of the global machine 'raised both economic and social problems, though obviously far more immediately troubling ones in some countries (eg Britain) than in others (eg South Korea).' The 1997 economic meltdown in South Korea, previously vaunted as a model by experts for so many years, opened up an uncomfortably large trapdoor over the yawning chasm beneath the global economy.

As a result even the world's economic thought police, the World Bank and the IMF, are having to take stock. Again, when Hobsbawm was writing in the early 1990s, there was no sign of this: the two institutions, he wrote, 'politically backed by the US, had pursued a policy systematically favoring free-market orthodoxy, private enterprise and global free trade, which suited the late 20th-century US economy as well as it had the mid-19th-century British one, but not necessarily the world. If global decision-making was to realize its potential, such policies would have to be changed. This did not look like an immediate prospect.'

Yet the shock to the system is such that even the World Bank seems now to accept that the policies of 'the Washington Consensus' since the 1970s – structural adjustment, privatization, deregulation – have been a failure. This has been obvious to any sensible observer for at least the last decade – if any national finance ministry had the record of consistent failure shown by IMF they would have been disbanded long ago. The Bank's former chief economist, Joseph Stiglitz, argues that the State must intervene to correct the market's shortcomings and that a successful economy and balanced society will see government playing a strong role in regulation, social security, health and education. This, he maintains, must form the core of a new consensus – a new economic agenda for the 21st century.

There are two perspectives on how and why the message has finally got through even to the pedlars of the original 'Washington Consensus'. The cynical response is that the 'change of heart' is simply because Western economists and financiers are concerned that shockwaves like those from East Asia in 1997 could actually bring their own houses tumbling around their ears rather than just the insignificant mud walls of the poor.

But the more positive response is that this is yet another example of where a long campaign of resistance has finally won its reward, where an apparently marginal idea has finally become the accepted wisdom of the mainstream. Popular protest and resistance can still make a difference, even in an age when politicians are more distrusted than they have ever been before. The fall of the Stalinist regimes of Eastern Europe shows this as clearly as it does Communism's failure: once public consent and willing obedience to their rule was lost, they melted away as quickly as snow in spring sunshine, for all their tanks and secret police.

Nevertheless the Myth of Progress still applies: we can no longer believe that humankind is spiraling ever onward and upward and must discard the idea of historical inevitability. Everything is now up for grabs. New, more equal and caring societies do not flow inevitably from the misshapen sluice gates of the old. On the contrary, people forge them and their wrong choices can take us two social steps back for every technological stride forward.

The world is ours to change – and if we do not change it, if we do not take up the relentless industrial railroad track and set it running in a new direction, then our descendants will reap a whirlwind that will make most of the events in history hitherto seem small.

Marking time: chronology
Some of the most important dates in human history.

Five million BC Australopithecus – the most human-like apes so far – emerge in Africa.

Two million BC *Homo habilis* (and his female companions) use their hands to make tools by chipping stones. Still only in Africa.

1.5 million BC *Homo erectus* and *femina erecta* take up the flame – literally, since they are the first hominids to discover fire.

800,000-500,000 BC The *erectus* hominids move out of Africa into Europe and Asia.

300,000 BC Our foremother, an African woman, gives birth to a DNAsty that includes us all.

40,000 BC Modern humans finally arrive on the scene and supersede (ie intermarry or wipe out) all the previous models.

40,000-10,000 BC Nomads cross the land bridges into Australia and the Americas. At the end of the last Ice Age the oceans rise and cut them off.

25,000 BC The first religion – worship of the Great Goddess Mother – spreads the world over.

9,000 BC Palestinian sheep are the first tamed farm animals – goats, pigs and cattle all follow.

8,500 BC The first fully domesticated crops are grown at Jericho in Palestine, and the first town grows up as a result.

6,500 BC The first agriculture emerges in the Americas, in the Andes.

4,000 BC The drying up of the Sahara forces people to migrate to the Nile region that will spawn the Egyptian civilization.

3,500 BC The first real civilizations emerge in Sumer and Egypt and the first rice is grown in China. The wheel is invented.

3,000 BC The great civilization of Harappa emerges in the Indus region of India – and sends ships across the Pacific. The first writing is developed in Sumer.

2,000 BC The Harappan civilization is destroyed as Aryan tribes invade India and found the Hindu religion.

1,800 BC Hammurabi consolidates the Babylonian empire.

1,700 BC The first Chinese civilization is ruled by the Shang.

1,600-600 BC Continual warring between the three great powers in the Middle East – Egypt, Babylon and Assyria.

1,500 BC Asians colonize the Pacific islands of Micronesia. The Hebrews invade Palestine.

1,200 BC The rise of the Olmecs, the first American civilization.

1,000 BC The Bantu peoples begin to spread over Africa. The Shang dynasty in China is conquered by Chou nomads, who establish the first feudal system.

800 BC Kush invades Egypt and rules it for a century.

771 BC China's Chou dynasty is overthrown.

729 BC Tiglath Pileser's army conquers Babylon to make Assyria the superpower of the day.

722 BC Assyria destroys Israel.

612 BC An alliance of Persians and Babylonians defeats the Assyrians and divides its empire.

604 BC Legendary date of Lao-tzu's birth.

567 BC The Hebrews of Judea are taken into Babylonian captivity.

551 BC The birth of Confucius.

538 BC Babylon is conquered by the Persian Empire of Darius I; the Hebrews return to Jerusalem with their Father God.

530 BC The Buddha reaches Enlightenment.

507 BC Athens becomes the first democracy.

450 BC The Olmec civilization is destroyed.

347 BC The Greek political philosopher Plato dies.

338 BC Philip of Macedonia conquers the rest of Greece.

334 BC Alexander the Great launches his conquest of Persia.

323 BC Alexander the Great dies; his empire is divided between four of his generals.

322 BC Chandragupta conquers northern India to establish the Mauryan Empire.
264 BC The First Punic War between Rome and Carthage begins.
257 BC The Indian King Asoka renounces warfare and embraces Buddhism.
241 BC Conscripted Roman farmers arrive home to find themselves landless.
221 BC China is united by the first emperor, Shih Huang-ti. The Great Wall is soon begun.
202 BC The Han dynasty is established in China.
146 BC Rome destroys Carthage
73 BC Spartacus leads a slave revolt against Rome.
49 BC Julius Caesar stages a military coup; Roman empire period.
AD 23 The Chinese capital Changan is sacked by nomadic invaders.
AD 30 Jesus Christ is executed.
AD 46 St Paul begins his missionary journeys.
AD 50 The rise of the African empire of Axum.
105 Paper is discovered in China
132 The Jews rebel against Rome; many are forced into exile.
150 Buddhism reaches China.
184 The revolt of the Yellow Turbans in China lasts 30 years.
200 The writing of the Indian classics, the *Mahabharata* and the *Ramayana*.
220 China's Han dynasty falls.
300 Bantu peoples settle in South Africa.
320 The Gupta dynasty in India is founded.
324 Constantine makes Christianity the official religion of the Roman Empire.
325 Axum destroys the Kushan capital Meroe.
410 Visigoths sack Rome.
425 Angles, Saxons and Jutes invade England.
451 Huns under Attila are defeated in Gaul but then sack Italy.
455 Vandals sack Rome.
476 Odoacer announces there will be no more Roman emperors.
520 Mathematic revolution in India: Aryabhata and Varamihara invent the decimal system.
600 The Mayan civilization in Central America reaches its peak.
622 Muhammad's *hejira*, his move from Mecca to Medina. The Islamic calendar dates from this year.
626 The T'ang dynasty, under the emperor Tai-tsung, revives Chinese art and religion.
632 Death of Muhammad.
641 Islamic armies conquer Egypt and attack the rest of North Africa.
645 Buddhism reaches Tibet.
650 Rise of the Huari civilization in the Andes.
651 Islam conquers Persia.
661 The Sunni and Shi'a branches of Islam split.
692 The Dome of the Rock is built in Jerusalem – the first great Islamic building.
700 The rise of Ghana's empire in West Africa.
732 Muslim forces are finally turned back in France.
750 Destruction of the Teotihuacan civilization.
800 Charlemagne sets himself up as Holy Roman Emperor.
850 Collapse of the Mayans.
853 China prints the first book.
900 Maori people sail from Tahiti and settle in Aotearoa (New Zealand).
912 The Norse Vikings conquer the north of France, which becomes Normandy.
963 Rise of the Toltecs.
1054 The Greek Orthodox Church in Constantinople splits from Rome.
1055 Turkish groups conquer Muslim Baghdad.
1076 Ghana falls to invasion.
1095 Pope Urban II calls the First Crusade.
1099 Crusaders capture Jerusalem, massacring Jews and Muslims alike.
1200 Rise of the empire of Mali.
1215 Genghis Khan's Mongols ravage Peking.
1260 Kublai Khan becomes Chinese emperor.
1300 The Yoruba city state of Ife rises to prominence. And the Italian Renaissance begins to blossom.
1315 Famine hits Europe.
1324 Kankan Musa, emperor of Mali, makes a pilgrimage to Mecca.
1325 The Aztecs establish their capital Tenochtitlán.
1341-53 The Black Death wipes out

millions in Asia and Europe.

1368 Chu Yuan-chang becomes the first Ming emperor of China.

1415 The Portuguese make their first conquest in Africa.

1425 The Shona king Mutota abandons Great Zimbabwe and begins to extend his empire.

1438 Pachacuti Inca leads a series of conquests to forge the Inca empire.

1453 The Ottoman Turks conquer Constantinople.

1455 The Pope gives his approval to the slave trade.

1492 Columbus strikes land in the Bahamas and Caribbean.

1496 Vasco da Gama sails to India and back to Portugal.

1500 Peak of the Benin empire in West Africa.

1502 Montezuma II becomes Aztec emperor.

1505 The Portuguese seize East African ports.

1510 The Portuguese begin shipping African slaves to Americas.

1517 Martin Luther challenges Church orthodoxy.

1519 Invasion of Aztec Mexico by the Spanish.

1526 Babur invades India to set up the Mughal empire.

1533 The Spanish conquer the Inca capital Cuzco.

1533 Death of Kabir Nanak, founder of Sikhism.

1546 The Mali empire is destroyed by Songhay.

1606 French settlers establish Quebec.

1619 Dutch take over the East Indies (Indonesia).

1620 The Pilgrim Parents arrive in New England.

1644 Suicide of last Ming emperor as rebels take Peking.

1649 British King Charles I is executed after a civil war.

1652 Dutch settlers arrive in South Africa.

1653 The Taj Mahal is completed.

1663 The Ottoman army is defeated at Vienna.

1715 Death of Louis XIV, France's 'Sun King'.

1739 The Persians sack Delhi.

1776 US Declaration of Independence from Britain.

1788 Arrival of the first British convict settlers in Australia.

1789 Revolution in France.

1791 French King Louis XVI is executed; France is at war with virtually all European powers.

1796 British conquer Ceylon.

1799 Napoleon's *coup d'état*.

1804 The murder of Tasmanian Aboriginals begins.

1807 The slave trade is abolished in the British Empire.

1808 Argentina becomes the first South American country to win independence from Spain.

1814 First permanent white settlement in New Zealand.

1815 The final defeat of Napoleon at Waterloo. The Congress of Vienna reimposes monarchy.

1818 Britain's East India Company becomes the effective ruler of India. Shaka establishes a Zulu empire.

1821 The fall of Lima to revolutionary forces and the declaration of Mexico's independence. The Maori civil wars begin.

1822 Brazil gains independence from Portugal. Liberia is set up as a country for freed slaves.

1836 South African Boers set out on their Great Trek north to escape British domination.

1840 Britain annexes New Zealand.

1842 Copper and gold are discovered in Australia. The First Opium War takes place between Britain and China.

1846 US conquers half of Mexico.

1848 The Year of Revolutions in Europe: the middle classes win a stake in political power. Marx and Engels publish *The Communist Manifesto*.

1854 Civil war in China ends with 20 million dead.

1857 Indians rebel against British rule but are suppressed after over a year's fighting – India formally becomes a British colony.

1860 France begins to build an empire in West Africa.

1865 The abolition of slavery in the US after a four-year civil war. Western powers forcibly open up Japan to trade; Japan launches into its miraculous modernization.

1867 Canada's federal constitution

defuses tension between its British and French communities.
1868 The Meiji restoration of the Emperor in Japan.
1871 Germany is united under the Prussian king and becomes Europe's most powerful nation.
1878 The European powers carve up Africa between them at the Congress of Berlin; Belgium's King Leopold is given Congo as a personal colony.
1890 The Lakota Indians are crushed by the US army at Wounded Knee.
1893 New Zealand women win the vote.
1898 Abyssinia defeats Italian colonizers at Adowa. Herzl calls for a Jewish national home.
1899 Britain starts the Boer War in South Africa.

And a slightly fuller version of the 20th century...

1900 The Boxer Rebellion of the Chinese against the Western powers.
1901 The unification of Australia.
1905 Japan defeats Czarist Russia, which is threatened at home by revolution. Einstein publishes his Special Theory of Relativity.
1910 South African independence entrenches white power. The Mexican Revolution begins.
1911 Nationalist revolution in China: the last emperor quits.
1914-18 First World War.
1915 c 1,000,000 Armenians killed by Ottoman Turks.
1917 Revolution in Russia: at first liberal democratic then the Bolsheviks assume power in the name of the working class.
1918 Socialist revolution is suppressed in Germany.
1920 The League of Nations is established. The first radio broadcasts take place.
1922 Mussolini and his fascists come to power in Italy.
1923 Power in Southern Rhodesia is given to white settlers.
1924 Lenin dies; Stalin beats Trotsky to the succession.
1926 Chiang Kai-shek's Nationalists unite China then turn on their Communist allies. Britain has a General Strike.
1927 The first talking pictures are

released.
1928 Agriculture is collectivized in the Soviet Union.
1929 The Wall Street Crash prompts the Great Depression.
1932 Thousands of peasant trade unionists are shot in El Salvador.
1933 Hitler becomes Chancellor of Germany – and sets up his first concentration camps. Roosevelt's New Deal combats depression with public works in the US.
1934 China's Communists live to fight another day by virtue of the Long March. Nicaraguan rebel leader Sandino is murdered by General Somoza.
1935 Stalin's Terror begins. Italy conquers Abyssinia (Ethiopia). A wave of strikes in Africa against colonial labor conditions. End of the Chaco War between Bolivia and Paraguay, which killed 100,000.
1936 Somoza seizes power in Nicaragua. The Left comes to power in Spain and Franco rebels: the Spanish Civil War begins. Germany occupies the Rhineland.
1937 Japan invades China. Leftists flock to defend the Republican cause in Spain.
1938 Germany occupies Austria. Britain and France hand over Czechoslovakia's Sudetenland to Germany in a peace agreement at Munich.
1939 Franco wins the Spanish Civil War and sets up a Fascist state.
1939-45 Second World War.
1940 The exiled Leon Trotsky is murdered in Mexico by Stalin's agents.
1942 The Warsaw Ghetto is attacked and thousands of Jews sent to concentration camps. Gandhi and Congress launch the 'Quit India' campaign.
1944 Famine in Bengal kills three million: Churchill directs grain elsewhere to help the war effort. The Bretton Woods Conference starts to plan the financial architecture of the post-War world.
1945 Stalin, Roosevelt and Churchill meet at Yalta to carve up the post-War world. The United Nations, World Bank and IMF are established. Cambodia and Vietnam declare

independence from France; Syria and Lebanon win independence from France.

1946 Civil war between Nationalists and Communists erupts in China. Ho Chi Minh's Communists win elections in the north of Vietnam.

1947 India and Pakistan win independence from Britain: 8.5 million become refugees and 400,000 die in inter-communal violence. The US offers aid to Europe in the Marshall Plan – but declares a crusade against Communism. Rebel leader U Aung San is assassinated in Burma just before independence.

1948 Gandhi is shot dead by a Hindu extremist. Palestine descends into civil war; Jews declare the new state of Israel. Independence for Ceylon (now Sri Lanka). Afrikaner Nationalists institutionalize apartheid in South Africa. The UN adopts the Declaration of Human Rights.

1949 Mao Zedong's Communists triumph in China. Independence for Indonesia and Laos. Germany becomes two countries, East and West.

1950 The Korean War begins as the North captures Seoul and the UN involves foreign troops. Jordan annexes the Palestinian West Bank. China seizes Tibet.

1952 The Mau Mau step up the battle to drive the British out of Kenya.

1953 The Korean War ends; two million died. Soviet tanks crush an uprising in East Germany.

1954 Nasser becomes Egypt's leader. Vietnam's Communist rebels defeat the French at Dien Bien Phu then take Hanoi. The CIA deposes President Arbenz of Guatemala; a military regime takes over.

1955 The Non-Aligned Movement is formed in Bandung, Indonesia. South Africa's ANC adopts the Freedom Charter. Sudan wins independence. US blacks boycott segregated buses, inspired by Rosa Parks.

1956 Tunisian independence. Nasser takes over the Suez Canal; Britain and France seize it back but are forced to hand it over to the UN. Hungary's revolt against Soviet rule is brutally put down.

1957 Six European nations form the Common Market. Independence for Ghana under Nkrumah and for Malaya.

1958 Algeria explodes as settlers support French rule. De Gaulle offers all African colonies independence or autonomy under France: only Guinea opts for independence.

1959 Castro's rebels topple the dictator Batista in Cuba. The Dalai Lama flees Tibet. Mao launches the Great Leap Forward in China.

1960 French Congo, Chad, Central African Republic, Togo and Madagascar gain independence from France; Nigeria from Britain. Lumumba wins independence for Congo from Belgium but is deposed by Mobutu. Ceylon's Sirimavo Bandaranaike becomes the world's first woman prime minister.

1961 In Congo Lumumba is murdered and UN Secretary-General Dag Hammarskjold dies in a plane crash. US invasion of Cuba's Bay of Pigs; Castro embraces Communism. Tanganyika (now Tanzania) wins independence from Britain under Nyerere.

1962 Algeria, Rwanda, Burundi, Uganda and Trinidad & Tobago gain independence. Nelson Mandela is jailed in South Africa. US and USSR dice with nuclear war over missiles in Cuba.

1963 The Organization of African Unity is formed. Kenya becomes independent under Kenyatta. US President Kennedy is shot dead.

1964 The Palestine Liberation Organization is formed. The US outlaws racial discrimination. Malawi and Zambia win independence.

1965 Indonesia's General Suharto seizes power: 700,000 leftists and community workers are murdered. US planes bomb North Vietnam. Singapore secedes from Malaysia. Rhodesia declares independence to retain white power.

1966 Mao launches the Cultural Revolution. Botswana and Lesotho win independence.

1967 Civil war in Nigeria over Biafran secession. Israel wins the Six Day War against the Arabs and captures Sinai, Gaza, West Bank and Jerusalem. Aboriginals win citizenship in Australia.

1968 Vietcong launch Tet Offensive; protest at US war in Vietnam all over the world. In US, Martin Luther King is shot dead. French students and workers take to the streets. Soviet tanks crush the Prague Spring in Czechoslovakia.

1969 British troops are sent into Northern Ireland. Four million face starvation in Biafra.

1970 Biafra surrenders in Nigeria. Intensive US bombing in Laos; Nixon sends troops into Cambodia. Fiji and Tonga gain independence.

1971 Bangladesh declares independence from Pakistan. Genocide ensues as Pakistani forces hit back but India helps the new nation into being. China takes Taiwan's seat at the UN. Bahrain wins independence.

1973 The last US combat troops withdraw from Vietnam. Lebanon plunges into civil war. Elected Marxist President Salvador Allende is murdered in a CIA-backed coup in Chile; massive repression follows. Egypt and Syria attack Israel but are defeated. Arab producers raise oil prices by 70 per cent, sending shock waves through the world economy.

1974 Ethiopian Emperor Haile Selassie is deposed. India joins the nuclear bomb club. US President Nixon resigns in disgrace.

1975 The extreme-Maoist Khmer Rouge take over in Cambodia. Vietnam is reunited as the North's forces take over the South. Mozambique, Papua New Guinea win independence. India's Indira Gandhi becomes repressive after resistance to mass sterilization. Morocco annexes Western Sahara. Indonesia seizes East Timor.

1976 In South Africa, mass protest against apartheid led by schoolchildren in Soweto. Mao Zedong dies.

1978 War between Ethiopia and Somalia. Israel and Egypt sign a peace treaty. Deng Xiaoping emerges as China's leader.

1979 The Shah of Iran is deposed; Ayatollah Khomeini leads a strict Islamic state. Cambodia is invaded by Vietnam and the Khmer Rouge

genocide revealed. The Sandinista revolution ousts the Nicaraguan dictator Somoza. Soviet troops install a new government in Afghanistan. Zimbabwe has black majority rule.

1980 Iran and Iraq go to war.

1981 Belize wins independence. Egypt's President Sadat and Bangladesh's President Ziaur Rahman are assassinated. Hundreds of thousands in western Europe demonstrate against nuclear weapons. The Solidarity union leads resistance in Communist Poland.

1982 Britain and Argentina go to war over the Falkland/Malvinas Islands. Israel invades Lebanon and holds the south. US-backed 'contras' invade Sandinista Nicaragua.

1983 Leftist Grenadan leader Maurice Bishop is murdered in a coup: US troops depose the new government. Mexico's debt crisis threatens Western banks.

1984 Indian leader Indira Gandhi is shot dead. US transnational Union Carbide's chemical leak at Bhopal is the worst industrial accident in history. Half a million die in famine in Ethiopia.

1985 Reformer Mikhail Gorbachev takes over in the Soviet Union. The Greenpeace boat *Rainbow Warrior* is blown up by French agents.

1986 Yoweri Museveni wins power in Uganda. Philippine President Marcos is ousted by people power; as is 'Baby Doc' Duvalier in Haiti. The Chernobyl explosion is the world's worst nuclear accident. 'Colored' people and Indians are given the vote in South Africa; Africans are not.

1987 Burkina Faso's inspirational leader Thomas Sankara is murdered. The USSR and US sign the first-ever treaty to cut nuclear weapons. Thousands of Chinese students demand more democracy.

1988 Soviet troops withdraw from Afghanistan. Benazir Bhutto of Pakistan becomes the first female leader of an Islamic country. The Iran-Iraq war ends. Yasser Arafat recognizes Israel.

1989 Paraguay's dictator Stroessner is deposed. Chinese students and workers occupy Tiananmen Square seeking more democracy but are brutally crushed by tanks.

Communist states in east Europe crumble one by one: Hungary, East Germany, Yugoslavia, Bulgaria and Romania.

1990 Namibia wins independence from South Africa. ANC leader Nelson Mandela is released from prison after 28 years. The USSR disintegrates as Latvia, Estonia, Lithuania, Uzbekistan, Moldova, Ukraine, Belarus and Armenia all declare independence. East Germans vote for a reunited Germany. Iraq invades Kuwait.

1991 Iraqi forces are driven out of Kuwait by US-led UN forces. Georgia and Azerbaijan declare independence from USSR. The Soviet Union is disbanded and Boris Yeltsin becomes Russian leader. Tigray-based rebels win power in Ethiopia. Croatia and Slovenia declare independence from Yugoslavia; war breaks out.

1992 Islamic fundamentalists take to arms in Algeria after an election they would win is cancelled. The Australian High Court recognizes Aboriginals' prior ownership of land. Long civil wars end in El Salvador and Mozambique. Bosnia declares independence from Yugoslavia; 'ethnic cleansing' of Muslims by Serbs begins. The Earth Summit in Rio is hamstrung by US negativity.

1993 Eritrea wins independence from Ethiopia after two decades of armed struggle.

1994 The Zapatista uprising in Chiapas, Mexico, protests the new North American Free Trade Agreement. 500,000 Tutsis are murdered by the majority Hutus in Rwanda in a horrifying genocide; rebel Tutsi forces take over and two million Hutus become refugees. Nelson Mandela is elected President of South Africa.

1995 The World Trade Organization (WTO) comes into being. A US-brokered peace deal splits Bosnia into Serb and Muslim/Croat parts.

1996 The Afghan capital Kabul falls to the extremist Taliban: women are banned from working.

1997 The dictator Mobutu is deposed after 32 years in Zaire/Congo. The Thai, Indonesian and South Korean economies all collapse – but are bailed out by the IMF. The Ottawa Treaty banning landmines is signed after a long campaign.

1998 Indonesian dictator Suharto is ousted after 32 years of power. Extreme weather conditions worldwide are blamed on global warming. Agreement is reached on an International Criminal Court and former Chilean dictator Pinochet is arrested in Britain. DR Congo descends into a civil war involving six of its neighbors.

1999 Nigeria embraces democracy. NATO bombs Serbia over ethnic cleansing of Albanians in Kosovo. Eritrea and Ethiopia fight a long and bitter border war. East Timor votes for independence but Indonesian militias take their revenge in a killing spree. A watershed anti-globalization protest scuppers the WTO meeting in Seattle.

Bibliography

Pelican History of the World, J M Roberts (Penguin, 1988). *A Women's History of the World*, Rosalind Miles (Michael Joseph, 1988). *Green History of the World*, Clive Ponting (Penguin 1993). *Progress and Barbarism: the World in the 20th Century*, Clive Ponting (Chatto & Windus 1998). *The Age of Revolution*, Eric Hobsbawm (Vintage 1996). *The Age of Extremes*, Eric Hobsbawm (Vintage 1996). *Africa in History*, Basil Davidson (Penguin 1984). *A Short History of the World*, HG Wells (Penguin 1922/1965).

Index

Bold page numbers refer to boxed text.

Afghanistan 129
Africa 14, 17, 68-75, 106-8; *see countries*
Americas:14-15, 60-7, 81-7; *see countries*
Angola 73, **119**
Aotearoa (New Zealand) 103-4, 106, 113, 129
Argentina 84
arts 33, 58
Aryans 23-4, 32
Asia 14, **56-7**; *see countries*
Australia 14, 102-3, 112
Austria 95, 111
banking systems 41, 100-1
Belgium 95, 96, 111
Brazil 66-7, 86
Britain 24, 42, 77, 97-9, 100, 101, 102, 106, 107, 108, 109, 111, 113, 117, 120
Canada 102, 112
Chile 64
China: (BC)19-20, 21, 25-8; (AD) 46-50, 89-91, 108-9, 111, **120**, 122
civilizations: Africa 17, 21, 68-72; Americas 60-5; China 19-20, 46-50; Greece 32-4; India 18-19, 50-1
class struggles: ancient Rome 35-6; Britain 99-100; France 92-3; Russia 114
colonial domination in: Africa 106-8, **119**; Americas 64-7, 81-2, 86-7; Australasia 102-6; India 108
Congo 68
crops, cultivation of 15-16
diseases 16, **54**, 65-6, 104, 105, 113
economic: depressions 118-20, 127-8; growth 135-6; inflation 38
Ecuador 64
education 99, 101, 110
Egypt (BC)17, 21, 25, 34
empires: early 22-6; Ghana 69; Greek 34; Mali 69; Mongol **56-7**, 60; Mughal 91; Ottoman **79**; Persian 25; Phoenician 22; Roman 35-8
environment, destruction of 133-4
Ethiopia **44**, 108, 122
Europe: (BC) 14, 23-4; (AD) 35, 37, 46, 52, **53**, 58, 76-80, 95-6; *see countries*
famine 54, 113, **119**, 120, 132
feudalism: China 25-6; Europe 52; Japan **89**
France: 76-7, 92-5, 96, 101, 109, 111, 117
Germany: 121-2, 96, 100, 111, 113, 117-18, 119, 121-2, 123, 127
Greece: (BC) 32-4; (AD) 96
Holland 76, 95, 106
human evolution/colonization 11-15
ideologies: Capitalism 118, 127, 134-5; Chartism 99; Communism 114, **120**, 136; democracy 32-3; Fascism 118, 122-3; Nazism 121-2, 123, 132-3
independence struggles: China 108-9; India 108; S. Africa 129-30; S. America 84-6
India: (BC)18-19, 24, 28, **31**; (AD) 50-1, 88, 91, 108, 112
Italy: 95, 96, 111, 118, 122; *see empires*: Roman

Japan: **89**, 109-10, 111, 121, 122
Jews 30-1, 122, 132
Kenya 68, 112
Kush **23**, **44**
labor, exploitation of 20-1, 26, 32, 66, 70, 78; *see class struggles and slavery/trade*
language, vernacular 59
Liberia 108
life, emergence of 10-11
Mexico 84-5, 120
Middle East (BC) 17, 21, 22, 25, 29
migration, rural/urban 16, 98, 101
monarchy 76-80, 95-6
Mozambique **119**
native peoples: Aboriginals 102-3; Amerindians 65; Maori 104, 106; North American Indians 81, 86-7; Zulus 106-7
nomadic peoples 22, 57, 63
Norway 95
numerical systems 51, 62
Pacific Islands **105**
philosophy 27, 33
Poland 95, 96
population 15, 50, 66, 89, 92, **123**
Portugal 66, 72-5, 86, 88, 105
printing 49, 58
racism 71, 107-8, 122, 132
religions: Aztec 63; Buddhism 28-9; Christianity 39-42, **44**, 52-9; Confucianism 27; Goddess worship **18-19**, 21; Hinduism 24; Islam 43-5, 54, 79; Judaism 29-31, 39; Taoism 27-8; Zoroastrianism 43
revolutions: French 92-3; Industrial 97-9; Maoist **120**; Russian 114-16
Russia/Soviet Union: 80, 95, 109, 110, 111, 114-16, 123, 125, 126, 127-8
science/technology 33, **41**, 97, 131, 133
Serbia 111, 132
slavery/trade: Africa **71**, 73-5, 106-7; ancient Greece/Rome 32, 36, 37; Brazil 66-7; United States **83**
South Africa 68, 106-7
South Korea 135
Spain 64, 66, 84, 95, 120, 122-3
Stone-Age culture 12-13, 14
Sudan **23**
Sweden 95
Switzerland 76, 129
time measurement 21
travel: rail 97, 111; road 25; sea 19
Turkey 55, 111, 132 *see empires*: Ottoman
United States 86-7, 95, 97, 100-1, 111, 113, 118-20, 121, 125, 127, 129
Venezuela 85
wars 23, 132: Americas 82-3; China 47; Cold War 126, 127; Crusades 54-7; England 47, 77; World Wars 111-12, 117, 122, 127
wealth: concentration 16, 38, 57-8, 70, 78, 92; redistribution 114-15
women 93: domination by men 30, 32, 34, 37, 52, 81, 99; power and status 12-13, 18-19, 21, 22, 27, 44; right to vote **113**, 129
writing 21, 23, 30, 32, 62, 105